P9-DBQ-445

SIMULATION GAMES

Design and Implementation

83311

Serdre est vivere

LIBRARY

SIMULATION GAMES
Design and Implementation

Robert Maidment

College of William and Mary

Russell H. Bronstein

Department of The Army,
Fort Monroe, Virginia

Charles E. Merrill Publishing Company
A Bell & Howell Company
Columbus, Ohio

LIBRARY

Published by
Charles E. Merrill Publishing Company
A Bell & Howell Company
Columbus, Ohio 43216

Copyright © 1973 by Bell & Howell. All rights
reserved. No part of this book may be reproduced
in any form, electronic or mechanical, including
photocopy, recording, or any information storage
and retrieval system, without permission in
writing from the publisher.

Library of Congress Catalog Card Number: 73-75051

International Standard Book Number: 0-675-08968-9

1 2 3 4 5 6 7 8 9 10 / 77 76 75 74 73

Printed in the United States of America

LB
1099
.S53
M34

To Clark C. Abt

Foreword

The professional book in education today seems to be written with one of two ends in mind. The author can try the "let's cover everything once over lightly" approach, or an author can choose to treat a single subject in depth. The first option tends to produce some familiarity with a range of trends and problems and procedures; it produces an ability to talk about a number of topics. The second option tends to produce depth of understanding, and understanding breeds enough confidence to carry a reader beyond a talking stage into an action stage. This book, *Simulation Games*, should create understanding, build confidence, and lead to action. It should inspire a reader to use and to create simulation games.

The highlight of *Simulation Games* is an actual game— "Pollution Control." The rest of the book revolves around the game spinning out a step by step, systematic approach to game processes, intricacies, and construction. The reader should follow the first three chapters in order, then should go directly to the appendix to read and, hopefully, play the game, and then should finish with the fourth chapter. There are two other steps implied by the intent of the authors: create your own games and use them.

The book is a positive pleasure to read and reflect on; the products of your reading and reflecting should be pleasure and reflective thinking on the part of your students.

John R. Lee
Northwestern University

Contents

APPENDICES

chapter one

Simulations, Games, and Simulation Games

Before presenting a detailed discussion of the design and uses of educational simulation games, it is appropriate to define our working terms. As the phrase implies, a simulation game possesses the characteristics of both a simulation and a game. We will examine the types of activities usually associated with simulations and with games and then demonstrate how simulations and games are interrelated as simulation games.

Physical Simulations

All simulations are based on a model. A model is a simplified but accurate representation of some aspect of the real world. Model cars and airplanes which clutter the bedrooms of young boys are perhaps the most familiar examples. Auto and aircraft manufacturers attempt to recreate the exterior reality of the car or plane by designing the parts to scale and by including

1

as much detail as possible. Other types of models with which educators, particularly physical science teachers, will be familiar are those portraying a physical system such as the atom or the solar system.

A model is static. Its components are fixed in place and are not designed to be moved. If we take the model and put it into motion so that its parts interact with one another as they do in real life, we have created a simulation. For example, an atom or a solar system model can be made into a simulation by attaching a small motor which causes the electrons to revolve around the nucleus and the planets around the sun.

Another more complex type of simulation is the flight simulator which is widely used in pilot and astronaut training programs. It too is based upon a model, but one considerably more elaborate than the examples discussed above. The simulator usually is composed only of the plane's cockpit and contains an exact replica of the instrument panel found in the actual aircraft. As the trainee "flies" the plane, the controls and instruments cause the simulator to react as it would during real flight.

The above examples demonstrate the varying degrees of complexity which can be built into a simulation. Usually the more complex a simulation is, the more closely it mirrors reality because the parts of the object the model contains are more accurately represented. For example, the flight simulator attempts to recreate the operations of the aircraft as closely as is technically possible. In order to accomplish this, all the variables that impact upon the performance of the plane must be included in the simulation model. It is a formidable task indeed considering the high degree of electrical and mechanical sophistication found in today's modern aircraft. The typical classroom simulation of the solar system also reflects reality, but to a lesser degree, since many parts of the actual system, such as individual asteroids, are omitted from the model. Of course we could make this simulation more real by adding these missing parts, but such an attempt would be infeasible, if not impossible, considering the thousands upon thousands of minute planetary bodies involved. But even if it were possible, would such an effort be worthwhile?

The answer to this question will depend upon how the

simulation is to be used. If we are training a pilot, it is of course important that he be able to cope with any eventuality which might occur during flight. The failure to include all aspects of reality in his training program might prove disastrous the first time he is confronted by an emergency for which he was not prepared in advance. The purpose of the solar system simulation, however, is quite different. The physical science teacher is not interested in a simulation which replicates every detail of the solar system, but one that demonstrates the position and movement of the sun and the nine major planets. The elimination of certain detail from the model, such as the asteroids, is not only tolerable but essential if the student is expected to focus his attention on the main features of the system without being overburdened with confusing detail.

Social Simulations and Simulation Games

Social simulations and simulation games are in some ways similar to physical simulations. Both are based on a model of some aspect of reality. The principal difference between the two is the type of reality being modeled. While the physical simulation is concerned with objects, the social simulation deals with people. Instead of constructing a model of the solar system or the atom, a designer of a social simulation will construct a model of a family, a legislature, an international community, or any number of other social institutions or systems. In place of representations of electrons, protons, and neutrons which comprise the atomic model, a social model will include representations of a father, a mother, a child, a legislator, a judge, or a nation. These individuals or groups can be represented by other persons or groups of persons acting out their roles as is the case in most classroom simulation games, or by mathematical symbols programmed into a computerized simulation model as is the case in simulations used in social science research.

The construction of even the simplest social model is much more difficult than the construction of physical models. Through precise mathematical calculation based upon physical laws, the exact position and motions of the planets can be accurately computed. Translating these calculations into a very realistic model is not terribly difficult. Human behavior, however, is not this easy to simulate. There are no laws of behavior now, and there probably never will be, which can be used to predict with accuracy the actions of individuals or groups within a particular social context. There are simply too many variables with which to contend.

Since social systems are far more complex than physical systems, they are understandably more difficult to model. The multitude of relevant variables makes it necessary to decide between those which are central to the model and those which can be safely discarded. Usually the more variables included, the more closely the model will duplicate reality. Take for example a city council. A very simple model would include a representation of individual councilmen with their roles limited to the formal act of voting upon specific pieces of legislation. But would a simulation based upon such a model be of any use? Probably not, because the legislative process in even the most fundamental lawmaking body is considerably more complex than this. Constituent and interest group pressure, the power, influence, and expertise of individual council members, the existence of a party system, and the input of relevant information for council use are essential factors and must be taken into account. The problem is to decide first, how real the simulation must be and second, to identify for inclusion in the model those variables needed to create the desired reality.

Social simulations used for educational purposes are usually presented in the format of a game. A game is usually defined as an activity involving interaction among individuals or groups who are attempting to achieve specific goals. The means for achieving these goals are limited by rules either formally stated or informally understood within the framework of the game. In addition to the common usage of this term to refer to such activities as football and chess, much of our everyday behavior also can be classified as games. Relationships among parents and children, employers and employees, elected officials and their constituencies are characteristic of social games.

A game situation occurs when individual actors or players within a system do not possess the capacity to achieve their goals alone. They are then forced to interact with one another in the hope of assembling the kinds of resources required for goal attainment. A resource is anything tangible or intangible which one actor finds useful in influencing the behavior of another actor for the purpose of achieving his objective. For example, money, social status, legal authority, and expertise are some types of resources that might prove useful in a social game.

Game activity usually takes the form of an exchange of resources. Take the very simple exchange which might occur between a businessman and a member of the city council. The businessman has the goal of preventing the enactment of a particular pollution control ordinance but does not possess the legal authority to block the legislation. The councilman has the goal of being reelected in the upcoming election but does not have sufficient funds with which to finance his campaign. In this case the businessman can use his resources to persuade the city council member to vote against the pollution control measure by threatening to withhold financial support during his upcoming election campaign. The city council member will probably be willing to exchange his vote for the businessman's pledge of financial support provided no other actor possessing greater influence objects to this course of action.

In many situations, however, an individual actor does not possess sufficient resources to influence the behavior of another. When this is the case, the logical strategy to follow is to form a coalition with other actors who are faced with a similar problem and who possess similar goals. For example, a group of actors alarmed at the high level of pollution in their community can band together and use their combined resources to persuade the city council to vote for a strict pollution control measure. These actors can threaten to withhold from individual council members such resources as money, favorable publicity, and votes necessary for reelection. Again it is likely that one or more of the city council members will exchange their votes for the resources needed for reelection.

In a game situation there exist certain rules that govern how resources may be used. The groups mentioned above could not physically coerce the city councilmen into voting for or against the pollution control measure because in the United States it is not permissible to use force to decide political questions. Those who want to effect change must channel their activities and resources through a political decision-making structure which is based upon both custom and law. If an actor does not obey the rules, he will be sanctioned and prohibited from further participation in the game.

A simulation game, as the name implies, contains characteristics of both a simulation and a game. It is an activity in which participants interact within an artificially produced environment which recreates some aspect of social reality. The participants, termed players, assume the roles of individuals or groups who exist in the particular social system being simulated. Their goals and those of the actors they represent are the same. Whether or not the players will achieve their goals will depend upon how successfully they plan their interaction strategy and use their resources. Specific rules are contained within the simulation game which govern the sequence and methods of interaction. These rules limit and guide behavior in a way that will insure that players experience success or failure in a manner similar to their counterparts in the real world who adopt the same goal attainment strategy.

A social game is translated into a simulation game by extracting the central aspects of the game from the larger social environment of which it is a part. The often unrecognized or undefined social rules which exist in a particular social situation are simplified and stated explicitly. The structure and design of simulation games will be discussed in greater detail in Chapter 4.

Replay

In conclusion, it should be noted that even among social scientists who work extensively with simulation techniques there do not yet exist agreed upon definitions of simulation, game, and simulation game. In view of this lack of conceptual clarity, it is not surprising to find these terms, as well as others such as gamed simulation or instructional simulation, used interchangeably throughout much of the social studies literature. In most cases where these terms are used, the authors are referring to the type of activity described above as a simulation game. However, it should be noted that there does exist a growing number of educational games which are not simulations of social processes or systems.[1] These nonsimulated games will not be dealt with in this volume.

The next chapter will help clarify the meaning of these terms by demonstrating how simulation techniques are used in both research and education and how simulation models are operationalized for these purposes.

---

[1] The reader who desires more information on nonsimulation games should see Layman E. Allen, et al "The Virtues of Nonsimulation Games," *Simulation and Games* 1, no. 3 (September 1970), 319–326.

chapter two

The History and Uses of Simulations

The Origins and Development of War Games

The ancestry of our contemporary instructional social simulations can be traced to the ancient game of chess which was probably first played in India about 1,500 years ago. In its earliest form the game was a crude attempt to simulate battle between two nations with the various game pieces representing competing forces possessing varying degrees of strength and flexibility. Until the eighteenth century such games were played primarily for enjoyment and for testing the intellectual and strategic skills of the opposing players. But during the Age of Enlightenment, as military men sought more rational means for planning the conduct and predicting the outcome of war, the potentiality of adapting chess-like games for serious military purposes first became apparent.

Throughout the nineteenth century Prussia pioneered the development and refinement of war gaming. The traditional chess pieces were discarded and replaced by pieces representing actual infantry, artillery, and cavalry units. Maps and terrain models of the proposed areas of combat replaced the checkered board and the rules governing the strength and movement of the various game pieces were more realistically prescribed. Teams of players replaced two single opposing players and judges or referees monitored the game activity to insure that the teams obeyed the rules of combat. These early war games were quite primitive when compared with those used by military planners today, but they did provide commanders with a tool which would be used to help predict the probable outcome of battle.[1]

While war games underwent further refinement during the first part of the twentieth century, it was not until after the end of the Second World War and the development of the computer that war gaming played an integral part in national security planning. Using simulated models, it became possible to analyze the increasingly complex military problems by electronically sifting through the masses of data.

Human players were replaced by programmed models which could be altered at will to test the feasibility of various policy alternatives. As war games increased in sophistication, so did the technical expertise required for their construction. Military planners found that the knowledge of social scientists, behavioral scientists, mathematicians, and computer programmers was as necessary as traditional military skills in designing computerized war games.

Social Science Simulations

While these developments were occurring in war gaming during the 1950s and 1960s, experimentation with other social simulations was taking place simultaneously. Because economists and business theorists already possessed clearly defined quantative models which could be easily translated into simulations, they took the lead in simulation design and use. But it was not long before political scientists, sociologists, and psychologists also discovered the research and practical values of simulation techniques. International relations simulations first began to appear in the mid-1950s. These simulations, originally developed by the RAND Corporation, were known as "crisis games" because they attempted to create possible

---

[1] Sidney F. Giffin, *The Crises Game: Simulating International Conflict* (New York: Doubleday and Company, 1965), 13–40.

future international crises in various parts of the world. The value of these types of simulations was that they provided foreign policy makers with a set of useable policy alternatives in the event similar crises actually would occur. A second type of international relations simulation was developed in the late 1950s and early 1960s by Harold Guetzkow and his colleagues at Northwestern University. Known as the "Inter-Nation Simulation," it did not simulate specific world crises, but rather recreated the main structural and dynamic features of the international system for the purpose of explaining the operation of the system and furthering the development of international relations theory.[2]

Since the early 1960s the number of policy planning and research simulations have increased at a rapid rate. In the policy areas, simulations have been designed to help local, state, and national governmental officials make more rational decisions in such fields as health care, transportation, welfare, fiscal and monetary planning, and, of course, the conduct of war. But in addition to their practical applications, simulations have also proven to be flexible research tools. The types of systems that have been subjected to research analysis using simulation techniques range from entire international systems to psychoanalytic theories underlying dreams.

Social theory construction and validation are two areas in which simulations have proven useful. When one designs a simulation, he is actually stating a theory in very concrete terms. He must identify the major actors in the system, specify the types of relationships among those actors, and locate relevant variables which affect these relationships. Also, simulation techniques can be helpful in validating a theory that has been stated verbally. If a simulation based on a particular theoretical model bears no similarity to the real world, the model probably lacks validity. The explanatory and predictive value of a theory can be tested by putting it into use.

All researchers like to operate with a controlled environment in which variables can be manipulated at will. Social

---

[2] Harold Guetzkow and others, *Simulation in International Relations: Developments for Research and Teaching* (Englewood Cliffs, New Jersey: Prentice-Hall, Inc., 1963); *see also* Herbert Goldhammer and Hans Speier, "Some Observations on Political Gaming," *World Politics* 12 (October 1959), 71–83.

scientists lack the type of laboratory conditions enjoyed by physical scientists because they must work with actors who interact with their environment in many different and complex ways. Under such circumstances, trying to isolate the underlying causes of events and the forces that govern an individual's or a group's behavior is quite a formidable task. For example, since it is not possible to study a state legislature under conditions which would allow the researchers to "play" with the individual legislators and the variables that affect their behavior, the social scientist must do the next best thing. He must create a simplified simulation of a legislature whose parts can be manipulated freely. Depending upon available resources and research aims, he can create a totally computerized simulation which contains no human players, a man-computer simulation which utilizes both human players and a computer, or a totally human simulation.

Regardless of the type of simulation employed, the findings of the social scientist will never equal the precision obtained by his colleagues in the physical sciences. Human behavior is much more complex than that of atoms or molecules. However, simulations are a useful tool for uncovering in social systems essential aspects which are often masked by the richness and complexity of the real world.[3]

Simulation Games in the Classroom

Growth and Development of Instructional Simulations

It was not long after early international simulations were first developed that some social science educators began to detect possible educational value in them. During the late 1950s and early 1960s, international simulation games were used in several undergraduate and graduate political science courses. While these early efforts met with some difficulties, most of

---

[3] Harold Guetzkow, Philip Kotler, and Randall L. Schultz, *Simulation in Social and Administrative Science: Overviews and Case Examples* (Englewood Cliffs, New Jersey: Prentice-Hall, Inc., 1972).

the users issued optimistic reports about the educational value of simulation games. They found that simulation techniques heightened motivation and interest and that students gained a greater appreciation of the complexities of the international system.[4]

Instructional social simulations first gained widespread popularity not at the college level, but at the elementary and secondary levels. Based on early enthusiastic reports praising the learning virtues of simulation games, educators and publishers began to devote considerable time and effort to designing, field testing, and marketing the games. Although later research indicated that some of these early findings were overly optimistic, the number of simulation games on the market continued to grow throughout the 1960s and early 1970s.[5]

The increasing popularity of instructional social simulations has been due partly to the enthusiasm that inevitably follows the introduction of a new and attractive instructional technique. History has clearly demonstrated that educators are as susceptible to the bandwagon effect as voters are at election time. Of equal importance has been the redefinition of the philosophy underlying social studies education. Emphasis has shifted away from the rote memorization of facts and principles. Instead, the focus is now on fostering an understanding of the structure and dynamics of political and social processes and developing problem-solving skills. Supporters of simulation games claim that these are the types of knowledge and skills best taught through simulation techniques. Whether or not simulation games actually live up to this claim will be the main point of discussion in the next chapter.

Classification of Instructional Simulations

Although there are many ways of classifying simulation games, for clarity we will use two: purpose and mode of operation.

---

[4] Lincoln P. Bloomfield, "Political Gaming," *United States Naval Institute Proceedings* 86 (September 1960), 57–64; see also Lincoln P. Bloomfield and Norman Padelford, "Three Experiments in Political Gaming," *American Political Science Review* 53, no. 4 (December 1959), 1105–1115 and Bernard C. Cohen, "Political Gaming in the Classroom," *The Journal of Politics* 24, no. 2 (May 1962), 367–81.

[5] The reader is directed to Appendix C for a partial listing of commercially produced simulation games.

Purpose. Social simulations that are used for instruction in elementary and secondary schools usually have one of three purposes: to prepare the student to assume a role he will someday have to play, or to better execute a role he is already playing; to teach the student about roles and processes that will affect his life, but in which he likely will not participate; and to teach the student about the courses and outcomes of certain historical events. In addition, there are general skills both cognitive and affective, that these three types of simulations foster.

Two examples of the first purpose are the simulation games "Generation Gap," which deals with conflicts and compromises between parents and children, and "Consumer Credit," which simulates the advantages and pitfalls of installment buying. Also included in the first category are numerous training simulations employed by government agencies and private industry for preparing employees for specific positions within their management bureaucracies. By placing the prospective employee in a simulated job environment, it is possible to observe and analyze his behavior, review his various areas of weakness, and point out expected difficulties with which he will have to contend. Simulations also have proven their value in teacher training programs by exposing the novice teacher to a wide variety of classroom situations, many of which he probably would not encounter in the traditional student teacher program.[6]

The second purpose for using instructional social simulations is perhaps best exemplified by the international relations simulation games presently being used in elementary and secondary education. It is unlikely that any of the students in a particular classroom will have to assume the role of the president or the secretary of state, but all students should assume the role of informed citizen and voter. To analyze effectively the policy decisions when they relate to foreign affairs as well as cast a rational vote on these matters, the individual must be aware of the problems faced by the nation's

---

[6] P. J. Tansey, "Simulation Techniques in the Training of Teachers," *Simulation and Games* 1, no. 3 (September 1970), 281–303.

decision makers and the types of forces which affect their choice of policy alternatives. The same argument holds true for the need to understand the functioning of state and local governments as well.

The teaching of historical events through simulation games has been quite popular in recent years. It is a means for making potentially uninteresting events come to life and for giving students a more direct understanding of the thoughts and actions of previous generations. Historical simulation games, like all simulations, present complex events to students, thus discouraging their acceptance of simple cause and effect explanations of the origins, courses, and results of past events. Two examples of historical simulation games are "Destiny," which attempts to recreate events as they occurred just prior to the outbreak of the Spanish-American War, and "Division," which deals with the complexities of American politics during the decade prior to the outbreak of the Civil War.

Mode of Operation. The second area of classification deals with the specific methods by which a simulation model is put into use. By far, the most common type of instructional social simulation is the "man simulation" which employs all human players and does not require computer assistance. Its relative inexpensiveness and adaptability to the traditional classroom setting accounts for the popularity of the simulation. Man simulations also possess the additional advantage of requiring interaction among the players. This advantage may be beneficial in developing such social skills as effective communication and techniques of competition and compromise. Man simulations vary widely in their degree of complexity. Some contain few explicit rules to limit player behavior and to structure the course of game events. Others are highly structured with the aim of recreating a particular event or process as realistically as possible. The design of man simulation games will be discussed in greater detail in Chapter 4.

"Man-computer simulations," although receiving much attention in social studies literature, are still not widely used for instructional purposes because the required computer equipment at the elementary and secondary school levels is very scarce. Their operation, however, is similar to the conventional computer-assisted instructional systems. The computer presents the player with a simulated problem, reviews his solutions, provides him with an analysis of his decision, and then furnishes him with a new problem to solve. The difference between a man-computer simulation game and computer-assisted instruction is that, in the former, the player does not attempt to master conventional subject matters, but tries to solve specific political, economic, or social problems within a simulated real world environment.

One example of a man-computer simulation game is "The Sumerian Game" used for teaching basic economic principles to sixth grade students. The game is set in the Neolithic Age and the player assumes the role of a national leader faced with a series of crucial economic decisions that affect the welfare of his nation. Other examples of man-computer simulation games are "The Sierre Leone Game" which simulates the economy of an underdeveloped nation and "The Free Enterprise Game" which deals with the economics of manufacturing and retailing.[7]

In the above examples, the player interacts with a hypothetical social environment rather than other players. However, man-computer simulation games are now being designed to permit the student to interact with other real players or with artificially created players. In both cases, the computer is still used to analyze and judge player moves. These new types of man-computer simulations present the game designer with some difficult problems such as attempting to communicate through a computer. This can be a slow and cumbersome process, subject to player error. The communication process becomes more rigid and lacks the expressiveness found in face to face contact. The attempt to create artificial models of real actors is also full of difficulties. The design of appropriate player models that are sophisticated enough to interact with

---

[7] Richard L. Wing, "Two Computer-Based Economics Games for Sixth Graders," *Simulation Games in Learning*, eds. Sarane S. Boocock and E. O. Schild (Beverly Hills, California: Sage Publications, Inc., 1968), 155–68; see also Leonard Jimmer, "Toy Store: A Computer-Based Educational Game," *Simulation and Gaming in Social Science*, eds. Michael Inbar and Clarice S. Stoll (New York: The Free Press, 1972), 223–44.

a human player in a realistic manner is not an easy task, especially when one considers the multitude of social and psychological variables that affect even the most basic human behavior.[8]

The widespread use of such sophisticated man-computer simulation games lies in the future. For the present, man simulation games will continue to dominate the instructional simulation scene.

Replay

During the last two decades both social science researchers and educators have explored extensively the uses of simulations. Today many different forms of individual and group behavior are being analyzed and interpreted by social scientists using a wide variety of simulation techniques. This popularity is evidenced by the increasing frequency of national and international conferences devoted solely to the exchange of information relating to social simulation and by the proliferation of articles appearing in the journals of many disciplines dealing with the subject.

Paralleling this rise in interest among researchers has been a corresponding increase in the use of simulations for instructional purposes. Educators have found that simulations create a learning environment which motivates students and which also exposes them to the complexity and dynamics of social systems. This increasing popularity among elementary, secondary, and college instructors, as well as among educators in government and business, has resulted in the development and marketing of scores of simulations dealing with many types of social topics.

---

[8] Stuart Umpleby, "The Teaching Computer as a Gaming Laboratory," *Simulation and Games* 2, no. 1 (March 1971), 5–25; *see also* Martin Shubik and others, "An Artificial Player for a Business Market Game," *Simulation and Games* 2, no. 1 (March 1971), 27–43.

chapter three

Simulation Games and Learning

In the last chapter, brief mention was made of the popularity of simulation games during the last decade. One of the reasons given for their popularity was the assumption that simulations were superior to conventional instructional methods in teaching the complexities of social life and in developing decision-making and other social skills. The purpose of this chapter is to examine the claims made for instructional simulations and to contrast these claims by presenting the views of skeptics who are less convinced of their educational value. But before beginning this discussion, it is important to describe briefly the state of simulation game research since much of this section deals with specific research findings.

Simulation Games and Educational Research

Many of those who question the educational value of simulations are skeptical due to insufficient evidence that demonstrates the superiority of simulations over conventional instructional techniques. When instructional simulations were first popularized during the early 1960s, some educators felt that a major breakthrough had been made in social studies education. As subjective opinion yielded to concrete research findings, excessive enthusiasm mellowed and the educational advantages of simulations were evaluated more objectively. In recent years, simulation game research has greatly expanded in quantity and improved in quality. Researchers are still hampered by the inability to define adequately the types of player behavior that simulations portray and in developing appropriate instruments by which that behavior can be measured. Lack of coordination among research efforts has resulted in a failure to achieve a consensus in conceptual definitions and in research methodology. Attempting to compare or verify research findings without first agreeing upon such fundamentals is a pointless endeavor. However, these are common problems that plague many researchers who are attempting to break new ground and explore essentially unknown territory.[1]

The state of simulation game research has been mentioned to emphasize that what is now known about the behavioral impact of simulations is still very tentative. It is possible that simulations influence yet unrecognized behavior.

Instructional Simulation
as a Learning Environment

Supporters frequently point to three advantages that simulations have over other teaching methods in creating a favorable learning environment: a new and non-authoritarian role for the teacher, a more realistic and relevant presentation of learning experiences, and an increase in student motivation and interest.

---

[1] Jerry L. Fletcher, "The Effectiveness of Simulation Games as Learning Environments: A Proposed Program of Research," *Simulation and Games* 2, no. 4 (December 1971), 425–454.

The Role of the Teacher

With instructional simulations, the teacher no longer assumes a dominant role in the learning process, nor is he the sole judge of the effectiveness of student behavior. The data source is not the teacher; it is the simulation game. The success or failure in choosing appropriate strategies is evidenced by whether or not a student has understood the system being simulated.

Although his role has changed, the teacher does not become a useless appendage in the classroom. He is no longer an authoritarian figure who acts as the fountain of all knowledge, but he still retains the important tasks of preparing the students to participate effectively in the simulation and of insuring that it runs smoothly. His post-simulation responsibility of discussing and analyzing with the students their behavior and the significance of particular events is of great importance. A detailed discussion of these tasks is included in Chapter 4.

The Presentation of Learning Experiences

With most types of classroom instruction there is often little connection between what occurs in the classroom and what is happening in the real world. Generally this is what is meant by the term "relevancy gap" which has been so widely publicized in recent years. Supporters claim that simulation games can bridge this gap by bringing a small and simplified slice of the real world into the classroom where it can be examined and experienced by students.

Learning by doing is the oldest educational technique known to man and is the philosophical base upon which instructional simulations rest. Such a philosophy generally has been accepted and practiced in the vocational arts and in the physical sciences, but until recently it has not been attempted in the social sciences. Most social processes occur outside the classroom, and in the past there were no practical means for first-hand examination. Although films and field trips have some utility in this respect, they do not allow the student to become an active participant. With instructional simulations, however, the student is able to experiment with a wide variety of roles in different social settings without having to face the consequences of faulty decisions. This advantage is similar to that of a military commander participating in a war game. Due to an error in his judgment, his simulated army might be wiped out, but no lives are lost and the commander learns a tactical or strategic lesson which may be useful later in actual combat.

Some of the harshest criticism leveled at simulation games involves the difference between simulated reality and actual reality. Some argue that because the degree of reality contained in a simulation is not the same as that found in the real world, students will acquire an oversimplified picture of the actual social process. Critics fear that students will erroneously assume that they can control the outputs of the real system as easily as they can control those of the simulated system and that this assumption will lead to frustration and disillusionment later in life. Others see a danger in allowing students to make decisions without having to suffer the consequences of their actions. In an international relations simulation game, a player can declare war and destroy other nations in a game context completely devoid of the actual horrors of war. Whether or not repeated involvement in instructional simulations leads to amoral or immoral behavior is still a question that cannot be answered with certainty.[2]

Motivation

In recent years educational critics have sharply attacked schools as being dull, joyless, unimaginative prisons that stifle student initiative, creativity, and motivation. Before most students will expend the effort to learn, they first must be convinced that the subject is worth their attention. Extrinsic rewards, such as grades and gold stars, might be effective motivators for some students, but certainly not for all. Even children who respond positively to these types of motivators

---

[2] Ivor Kraft, "Pedagogical Futility in Fun and Games?" *The Journal of the National Education Association* 54, no. 1 (January 1967), 71–72; see also William A. Nesbitt, *Simulation Games for the Social Studies Classroom*, 2nd ed. (New York: The Foreign Policy Association 1971), 54–67.

often will lose interest in the subject once they receive the reward. Unless there exists within the student the desire to learn based upon the belief that the material he is being asked to master will affect his life, much of the time and effort devoted to his education will be wasted.

Simulations can motivate students to learn because students deal with real roles and real problems instead of verbal abstracted descriptions of these roles and problems. The elements of competition, chance, and excitement are as evident in a simulation as in chess or football. Of course, there are some students who do not enjoy the required social interaction and competition involved in simulation play, and for these students simulations are threatening, rather than motivating, experiences. But this number generally comprises a very small minority of students.[3]

It is frequently accepted that simulations do indeed motivate student learning, but the major unanswered question is whether this effect is a result of inherent qualities contained in simulations or whether it is a temporary phenomenon engendered by participating in a new learning experience. It is possible that students will become bored with simulations after participating a few times just as they are presently bored with conventional instructional techniques.

Because the use of instructional simulations have temporarily demonstrated their ability to motivate students, many educators have been quite successful in using them with disadvantaged and underachieving students. Lack of motivation and interest is widespread among middle-class and upper-class students, but rampant among students in low socio-economic areas. Higher rates of failure and non-completion of school may suggest certain cause-effect relationships. Such students frequently lack the verbal skills needed to function effectively in the traditional classroom environment with its chronic emphasis upon reading and writing. Many of these same students, however, have participated quite effectively in instructional simulations and have displayed a wide variety of intuitive

---

[3] Sarane S. Boocock and James S. Coleman, "Games with Simulated Environments in Learning," *Sociology of Education* 39, no. 3 (Summer 1966), 215–236; *see also* Sarane S. Boocock, "The Life Career Game," *The Personnel and Guidance Journal* 46, no. 4 (December 1967), 328–334.

insights and analytical skills.[4] These preliminary successes indicate that simulations might be useful instruments for uncovering aptitudes and abilities that have been buried beneath layers of indifference and apathy.

Many educators have found that participation in simulation games increases students' general interest in the subject. This is evidenced by their willingness to seek additional information outside the classroom on their own. Whether this increase in interest is permanent or only temporary remains to be seen.[5]

What is Learned?

Considerable disagreement exists over what simulation games teach and how well they teach it. Many of the claims made for simulations have not been subjected to objective empirical examination. When they have been examined, the findings have led to conflicting conclusions.

Knowledge

Facts and Principles. While instructional simulations have been used successfully to teach facts and principles, they have not been found to be superior to more conventional techniques. If the aim of the teacher is to limit his instruction to specific subject content only, he probably would be wise to avoid the use of instructional simulations because of their cost and the

---

[4] Clark C. Abt, *Serious Games* (New York: The Viking Press, 1970), 61–78; *see also* Elliot Carlsen, *Learning Through Games* (Washington, D.C.: Public Affairs Press, 1969), 109–140; Dale C. Farran, "Competition and Learning for Underachievers," eds. Sarane S. Boocock and E. O. Schild (Beverly Hills, California: Sage Publications, Inc., 1968), 191–203; Larry A. Braskamp and Richard M. Hodgetts, "The Role of an Objective Evaluation Model in Simulation Gaming," *Simulation and Games* 2, no. 2 (June 1971), 197–212.

[5] Wentworth Clarke, "A Research Note on Simulation in the Social Studies," *Simulation and Games* 1, no. 2 (June 1970), 203–210; *see also* Samuel A. Livingston, "Effects of a Legislative Simulation Game on the Political Attitudes of Junior High School Students," *Simulation and Games* 3, no. 1 (March 1972), 41–51.

amount of time ultimately required for student preparation and participation.[6]

System Structure and Dynamics.   Although simulations may not be the best means for teaching facts and principles, their supporters claim that they can be used to good advantage in teaching the structure and operation of social systems. A social system is best understood by seeing it as a dynamic, integrated whole, not by examining its isolated individual parts. For example, the student may find it difficult to understand how a legislature functions by studying separately the party organization, the committee system, the leaders, the legislators, and the rules governing legislative procedure; but given an opportunity to participate in a simulated legislature, he will see how these different variables mesh and impact upon one another in diverse and complex ways.[7]

Some educators believe that the best way for students to learn about the complexity of social systems is by encouraging them to design their own simulation game. In designing a game, they must identify the game actors and their resources and goals, and state clearly the methods by which the actors will interact to reach their goals. Students probably gain a more thorough understanding of how a social system works by designing their own game than by participating in a game developed by someone else.

Skills

Decision-Making and Analytical Skills.   The success of the student in a simulation game will not depend upon how well

---

[6] Cleo H. Cherryholmes, "Some Current Research on Effectiveness of Educational Simulations: Implications for Alternative Strategies," *American Behavioral Scientist* 10, no. 2 (October 1966), 4–7; *see also* Sarane S. Boocock, "An Experimental Study of the Learning Effects of Two Games with Simulated Environments," *American Behavioral Scientist* 10, no. 2 (October 1966), 8–17; James A. Robinson and others, "Teaching with Inter-Nation Simulation and Case Studies," *American Political Science Review* 60, no. 1 (March 1966), 53–65.
[7] Abt, *Serious Games,* 15–34; *see also* Alice Kaplan Gordon, *Games for Growth: Educational Games in the Classroom* (Palo Alto, California: Science Research Associates, Inc., 1970), 26–32.

he is able to memorize facts and principles, but upon how successfully he can analyze information to arrive at rational decisions. Because a simulation is a dynamic process, the student must continually plan, make decisions, analyze feedback, and replan as the simulation progresses. One of the principal attributes assigned to instructional simulations is their ability to develop general decision-making skills which are beneficial in a wide variety of social situations. However, much of the evidence that supports this claim is based upon opinion and not upon solid research findings.

Social Skills. Many sociologists and anthropologists have commented upon the importance of games in the process of socialization of children. Through play activity children are introduced to such elementary social skills as communication, cooperation, competition, and understanding of social rules.[8] Advocates claim that instructional simulations which require player interaction can further the development of these skills under relatively controlled classroom conditions. The student can learn through simulations that cooperation as well as competition often is needed to obtain desired goals. He must learn to communicate his ideas and opinions to his fellow players in a coherent manner in order to persuade them to his views.

Attitudes

Some, but not all, educators have found that instructional simulations can bring about a change in player attitudes relating to the simulated system itself or to particular roles within the system. Shifts in attitudes have been reported from simulations dealing with race relations, international relations, and the legislative process.[9]

---

[8] Clarice S. Stoll and Michael Inbar, "Games and Socialization: An Exploratory Study of Race Differences," *The Sociological Quarterly* 2, no. 3 (Summer 1970), 374–381.

[9] *Simulation and Games* 3, 41–51; see also *The American Political Science Review* 60, 53–65; *American Behavioral Scientist*, 10, 8–17; Paul DeKock, "Simulations and Changes in Racial Attitudes," *Social Education* 33, no. 2 (February 1969), 181–183.

An increase in feelings of efficacy or an individual's belief that through his actions he can affect the workings of a system has been reported to occur while playing many simulations. This related change may result from obtaining an understanding of the various ways that component parts of the system fit together and the ways that they can be manipulated to affect the system's output. A weakened society may result from feelings of helplessness in the face of social forces that are beyond an individual's comprehension or power to affect. There are indications that simulations can be beneficial in reducing such negative feelings and in increasing an individual's social self-confidence and willingness to become involved.[10]

Replay

The final verdict relating to the value of simulations as instructional tools has yet to be delivered. From what is now known, it appears that the principal strength of simulation games is found in their ability to motivate student learning. But there are also indications that instructional simulations impart some types of knowledge and skills and effect attitudes and beliefs more successfully than do many conventional methods of instruction. However, it must also be noted that some researchers have arrived at generally negative conclusions regarding the supposed attributes of simulation games. In addition, there is an increasing feeling among many reputable educators that methodology is not the major factor in determining success or failure in the classroom; rather, the degree of success will depend upon the skill and experience of the teacher.

The discovery of new uses for simulation games is a distinct possibility as educators become more familiar with their impact on student behavior. As mentioned earlier in the chapter, simulations could prove useful in measuring aptitudes among those frequently handicapped by the conventional testing environment. Simulations might also be employed as a

---

[10] *American Behavioral Scientist* 10, pp. 8–17; *see also Simulation and Games* 3, 41–51.

psychological tool to help determine the emotional strengths and weaknesses of students in a variety of different social situations. But the implementation of these applications lies in the future. For the present, simulation games are a promising, but not totally proven instructional technique useful for gaining student interest and enriching the social studies curriculum.

chapter four

The Design and Use of Classroom Simulation Games

The purpose of this chapter is to provide a general outline of the necessary procedures for planning, designing, and administering simulation games.

Determine the Appropriateness of a Simulation Game Approach

Many teachers choose to use a simulation game without first considering whether or not it is the most effective and economical means for achieving course objectives. Little or no relationship between the game and the course objectives can be the result of a forced introduction into the school curriculum. Before deciding upon a simulation game approach, the teacher should carefully examine the advantages of the simulation game as a total learning technique. The most efficient and effective types of knowledge and skills it teaches should also be looked into. Then, based upon student needs and course

29

objectives the teacher can decide if the simulation game approach is most effective.

The Commercial Versus the Self-Produced Game

Once the teacher has elected a simulation game approach to help achieve course objectives, he must next decide what type of game to use. He may use a game available on the commercial market or design and construct a game and tailor it to his own specific needs.

Commercially distributed promotional materials seldom identify game objectives clearly. The teacher must make every effort to examine a simulation game prior to purchase to determine what the students will gain from participation and insure that students have the ability to play it effectively. If the simulation being considered for use is not available locally, it is sometimes possible to purchase single copies of the instructor and player manuals from the publisher.[1]

The use of a commercial simulation game has two principal advantages. First, its use saves the teacher considerable time and effort. Game design is a time-consuming process that requires many hours of imagination and industry. Even professional game designers with many years of design experience find that their products often have to be reworked several times before they are suitable for use in the classroom. If the teacher hopes to involve the students in the design process in conjunction with a particular course, the problem of time becomes even more acute since considerable classroom time is required for research and design.

A second advantage is that commercial games usually are designed by individuals possessing considerable expertise both in the specific topic being simulated and in general game construction. These games are usually field tested to insure their playability and validity before they are packaged and placed on the educational market.

The major disadvantage of using a commercial game, and

---

[1] A useful scheme for evaluating commercial simulation games is found in Judith A. Gillespie, "Analyzing and Evaluating Classroom Games," *Social Education* 36, no. 1 (January 1972), 33–42.

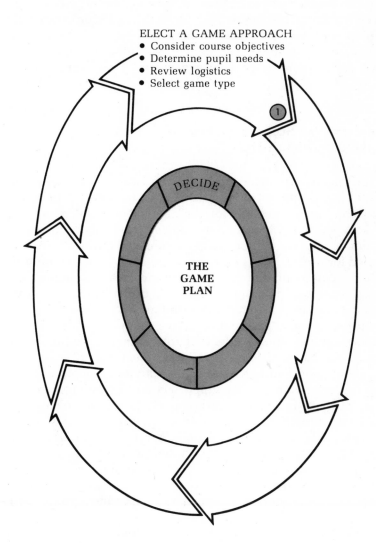

SELECT A GAME APPROACH
- Consider course objectives
- Determine pupil needs
- Review logistics
- Select game type

DECIDE

THE
GAME
PLAN

one which many educators feel outweighs the two advantages mentioned above, is that its use deprives both the students and the teacher of the important learning experience of constructing the game themselves. As was suggested earlier, the student will probably learn more about the structure and dynamics of a particular process by designing and playing his own game, than by playing a game which is commercially designed.

Determine the Scope and Objectives of the Simulation Game

If the teacher has decided to design a simulation game either alone or with the aid of his students, his next step is to outline the scope and objectives of the game. The game must help to achieve at least one of the objectives of the course. For example, the simulation game "Pollution Control" was designed for use in a 12th grade course entitled "The Community" which dealt with the demographic, political, economic, and social aspects of community life.[2] One of the course objectives was to familiarize the students with the political decision-making process while a second objective was to provide a deeper understanding of the problems of environmental pollution. The game was designed to achieve both objectives.

The general outline of the game activity involves pollution control legislation and its supporters and opponents who are attempting to persuade a city council to decide the issue in their respective favors. The political decision-making process enables students to follow the path that individuals and groups must follow in trying to influence political outcomes. In addition, the game players are required to analyze the available information on pollution control and formulate specific policy proposals. This game is an appropriate learning activity in the course for which it was designed.

After the scope of the proposed simulation game has been determined, the designer should formulate a list of tentative

---

[2] Attention is invited to Appendix A which contains the complete game entitled "Pollution Control." Subsequent material describes the key steps in preparing such a game for classroom use.

game objectives. These objectives can be related to specific game content or to more general attitudes and skills. In deciding upon these objectives, the teacher must remember to measure his students' attainment later in the course. Since educational researchers only recently have begun to investigate the ways in which student behavior during simulation game play can be measured, the classroom teacher will have to use his imagination in developing appropriate evaluation techniques and measures. An examination of recent simulation game research will prove helpful in providing suggestions.

The teacher should realize that the objectives he formulates in the early stages of game design may prove to be only temporary. During the design process he may discover that one or more of his original objectives cannot be achieved through game play. New objectives may suggest themselves as the teacher becomes more familiar with the design process and the material itself.

Determine
Required Data

Types of Data

In designing a simulation game that deals with any social process, the teacher should identify the actors who participate in the process, the goals, and the means by which they attempt to achieve these goals.

If the students are to be involved in the design activity, they should first be provided with a brief orientation involving the general theory underlying simulation game design and the educational uses of simulation games. Such an orientation will aid the students in understanding the purpose of their activity. In addition, students would benefit by examining simulation games produced commercially or locally so they can visualize the end product.

Data Sources

There exists a wide variety of information sources available to teachers and students. Personal experience can be a valuable

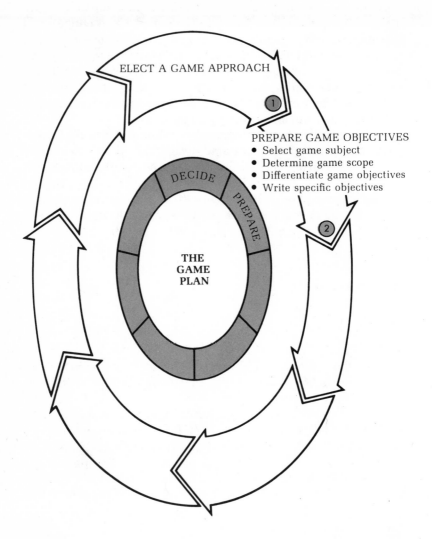

ELECT A GAME APPROACH

PREPARE GAME OBJECTIVES
- Select game subject
- Determine game scope
- Differentiate game objectives
- Write specific objectives

DECIDE

PREPARE

THE
GAME
PLAN

source if the game designers have participated in the process being simulated or have seen the process in action. For example, if an activity within the school system is being simulated, the students and teacher can provide most of the information required for the game design.

The sources most commonly used by simulation game designers include books and periodicals. Unfortunately, scholarly journals and most of the published materials which are particularly useful are not available in schools or local public libraries. However, if a college or university is located nearby, its library should certainly be explored as a source of appropriate material.

Since the authors are attempting to explicitly define the relationships among the variables of the system under study, the most valuable sources of information are those that attempt theoretical explanations of social phenomena. Because a social model is based upon certain theoretical assumptions, the discovery of a theory relating to the process being simulated in the classroom can be a fruitful beginning in developing the game model. However, the teacher should caution his students against assuming automatically that the existence of a theory equals an accurate explanation of the real world. Old theories are continuously being revised or discarded as their explanatory power is found to be lacking. The game designer will find that in many areas of the social sciences there can exist two or more conflicting theories that attempt to explain a single social phenomenon. Since many teachers and students have neither expertise nor time to evaluate the validity of opposing theoretical arguments, they probably will find it best to base their game on the theory most widely accepted at the time.

While source materials that deal with social theory are often the most valuable in simulation game design, they are frequently the most difficult to read and digest, particularly for secondary school students. The more traditional descriptive works that are easy to understand can provide students with valuable data on the identity of the actors, their goals, and their resources. In designing "Pollution Control," for example, a number of very useful descriptive works were located that provided the students with a general structure of the decision-making process within the community. These general works were supplemented with case studies involving different ways in which the problem of pollution control was handled. These case studies helped to identify the actors who were involved in community decisions and how they influenced the decisions of the local government. However, when it came time to detail the interactive process, the information obtained from the more theoretical material proved extremely useful.

Personal experience, theoretical explanations, and traditional descriptive information found in books and periodicals can be coupled with student field research in data gathering. If, for instance, the local government had recently considered the problem of pollution, students could contact the participants and ask them to recreate their roles in the final decision.

Design the
Simulation Game Model

After all the data have been collected, the teacher is ready to begin the actual design process. As mentioned earlier, all simulation games are based on a social model which is a simplified representation of some aspect of the social world. The teacher must decide how simple the model of the social world should be for his particular game as he begins construction. A simulation game which is based upon a complex model containing most of the system's variables will present the world in a more realistic manner than one based upon a model in which many of the variables are absent. However, the use of a complex model with many variables may result in a simulation game that is very difficult for the students to play. The central aspects of the simulated system are frequently lost in a game of such complexity. Conversely, a game based upon a model which is too simplified will give the students the impression that the process is much less complex than it is; and as stated earlier, much of the criticism that has been leveled at simulation games has to do with oversimplifying the complexities of the real world. The game designer must find a happy medium between developing a game that accurately reflects the structure and dynamics of the social process, and one that is playable and possesses educational value.

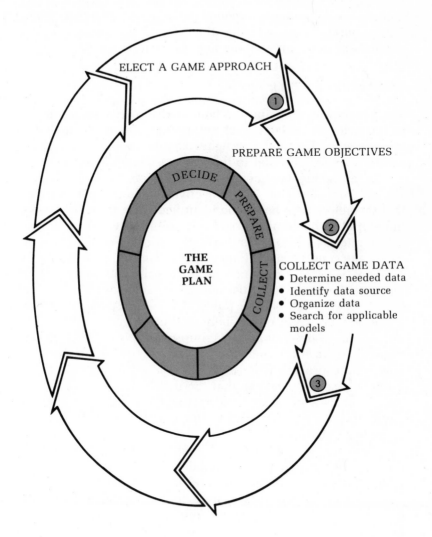

ELECT A GAME APPROACH

PREPARE GAME OBJECTIVES

DECIDE

PREPARE

THE
GAME
PLAN

COLLECT

COLLECT GAME DATA
● Determine needed data
● Identify data source
● Organize data
● Search for applicable
  models

The Components of the Simulation Game Model

In designing a model for a simulation game, the teacher must include the following components: the actors and their goals, the resources possessed by the actors, the sequence and methods of actor interaction, and the criteria for winning.

The Actors and Their Goals

The process of reducing the complexity of the social model begins with the selection of actors who are to be included in the game. The game designer should include only those actors who are essential to the process being modeled.

In designing the model for "Pollution Control," it was known from the scope and objectives of the proposed game, that the actors who had to be identified were those who were influential in deciding the issue of pollution within a typical community. No theory dealing with pollution control was located, and general community political decision-making theory was not very helpful since political scientists were not in agreement over the identities of relevant actors within a typical community. Some believe political power is concentrated in a few actors, while others believe that power is widely dispersed among individuals and groups who specialize in specific issue areas. In the former theory, few participate in the decision-making process, while in the latter many participate. Other political scientists believe that the power structure of a community forms a spectrum ranging from those communities with "monolithic" characteristics to those with "pluralistic" forms of power structures.

Case studies were then selected to provide the necessary data for the construction of a model. From these case studies, it was possible to discern several possible game actors, but incorporation of all these actors in the model would have created a simulation game too complex for classroom use. The first group of actors not included in the model were those outside the community who often influenced pollution decisions within the community, but were considered nonessential in illuminating the basic features of the community decision-making process. Two examples of such actors were state and federal government officials, who often exert considerable influence on local pollution decisions through legislation and regulatory action. A second group of actors excluded from the model were those who only occasionally involved themselves in such issues. Finally, the third group not included were those who frequently participated but exerted little influence on the decisions.

The groups finally selected for inclusion in the model were those that exerted considerable influence in many different types of communities. Ad hoc groups of citizens, who were personally affected by the pollution or concerned in general about the adverse effects of pollution, were proponents in the legislation. The industry that caused the pollution was also an influential group. This group usually opposed any pollution control measure that would lower their level of production and decrease their profits. A third group of actors consisted of various community organizations that exerted considerable influence in deciding the issue, but who initially could not be classified as proponents or opponents. Their positions were decided as they became aware of the issues and the consequences of the various actions. The fourth actor included in the model was the general public. Except in those communities using the referendum, the unorganized general public had little direct influence on the decision-making process. The public did, however, exert indirect influence through control of the vote. The fifth and final group of actors included in the model were the members of the city council. This group had the final authority to decide whether or not a pollution control ordinance would be enacted.

It should be noted that the general public and the city council have no roles in the simulation game. The fact that an actor is essential to the operation of a model does not necessarily mean that his role has to be acted out by a student player. The actor's response to the moves of the other players can be included in the rules of the game. An examination of the rules for "Pollution Control" will reveal how this was accomplished for the general public and the city council.

The rules of the game that apply to the general public and the city council are referred to as "environmental response rules" because they determine how a player's hypothetical social environment will react to his moves. These rules are used when the designer decides that the game will operate more effectively and with less complexity by predetermining certain actor responses. Environmental response rules determine how an actor will respond in a given situation. For example, in "Pollution Control" it is assumed that the members of the city council will automatically respond to the demands of those community members who exert the most influence upon them. This oversimplification illustrates the way city councilmen make decisions. However, other factors, such as ideological beliefs, also influence their decisions. In reality, politicians should not be perceived as being manipulated by the most influential individuals and groups within the community.

While the use of environmental response rules are a useful device in game design, they also complicate game construction. The designer must have some basis for predicting how actors will respond in given situations. If all actors are represented by student players, the problem is eliminated because each player will determine his own response to game events. Teachers who are experimenting with simulation game design may wish to avoid the use of a complex series of environmental response rules, unless they are basing their game on an already existent model that explicitly describes actor behavior.

The teacher should carefully and accurately state the actor goals. If an actor is assigned an incorrect or illogical goal, there will be little or no connection between his behavior in the simulation game and the behavior of the actor in real life. Again, it should be noted that the selection of a single goal for each actor is an oversimplification of reality. Many actors have multiple and sometimes competitive goals. But the incorporation of more than one goal in the model may result in a simulation game of too great a complexity.

Actor Resources

Whether or not an individual or a group are able to achieve their goals partially depends upon the type and quantity of resources they possess. A resource is any commodity or personal attribute that is useful to an actor in the attainment of

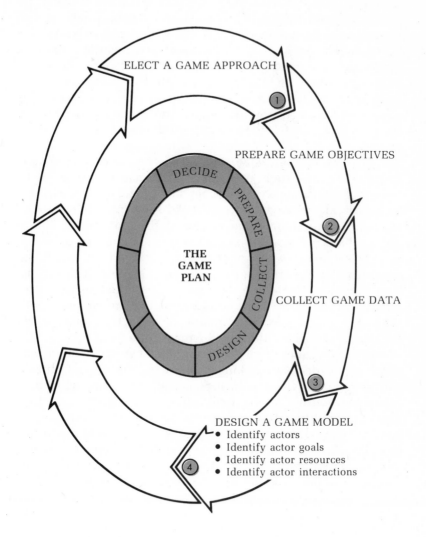

his goals. The game designer must first identify these resources then express them in concrete terms. Many theoretical works dealing with a particular social process describe explicitly the resources used by the individuals and groups involved. For example, in designing the model for "Pollution Control," it was learned that political scientists have identified about a dozen political resources such as wealth, reputation, social status, and the vote that are used in the decision-making process. Interviews with those involved in the actual process being simulated can also provide useful information about the resources they have found to be important in determining behavior.

In a simulation game, the actors' resources are usually apparent so that their use and transfer can be observed by the game participants. The teacher should attempt to distribute resources to the model actors in the same proportion found among the individuals and groups in the real world. This is not a difficult task when dealing with such tangible resources as physical objects and money. When working with such intangible resources as reputation and social status which are not easily defined, the game designer is presented with a more difficult problem. In "Pollution Control," no attempt was made to assign actors specific amounts of each type of resource because doing so would have increased the complexity of the model without gaining any corresponding benefit. In the second stage of the decision-making process in "Pollution Control," the actors are divided into three categories according to their levels of resources. In the final decision-making stage, the total amount of political resources possessed by each actor is represented by individual resources scores. It should be noted that the allocation of resources in this game was based upon very general assumptions about the most influential community members in deciding the pollution question.

Actor Interaction

The behavior of any individual or group involved in a goal-directed social activity is constrained and channeled by certain rules. These rules are either incorporated in the actor himself or imposed upon him by outside social forces. The task of the game designer is to identify the most important rules in the activity, and then find some means for reducing their complexity for inclusion in the game model.

Internal behavioral constraints usually spring from the personal attributes of each actor and include his goal. The external constraints are found in the surrounding social environment. Each social situation contains a different set of behavioral rules that prescribe how the actor must act if he hopes to successfully attain his goals. For example, groups that attempt to persuade a city council to enact certain pieces of legislation must involve themselves in the community decision-making process. This process, even in the smallest community, is very complex and includes a multitude of rules that guide and limit the behavior of the participants. In designing the model for "Pollution Control," this process had to be greatly simplified and only those rules that were deemed essential were included.

One of the most important rules in the "Pollution Control" game model was that which prescribed the sequence of events. As the reader examines the game, he will note that it has been divided into four distinct decision stages, an obvious oversimplification of the true complexity of community decision-making. In real life, social processes seldom develop in clearly defined stages visible to the participants. But the activity in a simulation game must be structured by generating certain simplifying assumptions about the flow of events in real life. Such assumptions were also made about the way real individuals and groups interact with one another during various decision stages. In "Pollution Control," the behavior of the general public and the city council depends solely upon the actions of the various community groups. Both are represented as mindless entities that simply react to the demands of the community's influentials. While this, too, is an oversimplification of the way in which the general public and a city council would actually behave, the assumption was considered sufficiently valid for use as one of the basic rules governing the interaction process.

A different kind of rule limiting player behavior and interaction is found in Stage 3 of the game. The ability to formulate specific policy proposals depends upon the possession of certain kinds of knowledge which is not widely distributed within the community. In "Pollution Control," it is assumed that only the Ad Hoc Committee and the Wilson Lumber and Paper Company possess sufficient expertise to participate in this stage of the decision-making process.

The problem faced by the designers at this point was that the student players would not have the same degree of knowledge as their counterparts in the real world. They would not be aware of the variety of policy alternatives available nor the consequences that would result from their enactment. It was decided, therefore, to provide an established list of alternatives from which the members of the Ad Hoc Committee and the Wilson Lumber and Paper Company could choose. In this way, the players would be provided with a common fund of knowledge essential in the particular game situation. Unlike the real world, where political actors must formulate their own policy proposals, in "Pollution Control" this task was accomplished for the players by the game designer.

Thus, in "Pollution Control," simplifying assumptions incorporated in the rules were used to decrease the complexity of the game. The game designer must insure that in diminishing the complexity of his game, he retains valid assumptions on which to base his rules so player reactions will be realistic.

Means for Determining the Winner

In some simulation games, there are specific criteria for determining the winner of the game that is usually decided by the number of points accumulated at the end of the game. In some games, however, such criteria do not exist and each player must evaluate his position, or the position of his team at the end of the game. "Pollution Control" could have contained a scoring system based upon points awarded for policy alternatives enacted, but it was felt that in this game such a scoring system would reduce player initiative and flexibility, as well as assign unrealistic win criteria to community groups that were given very general social and economic goals.

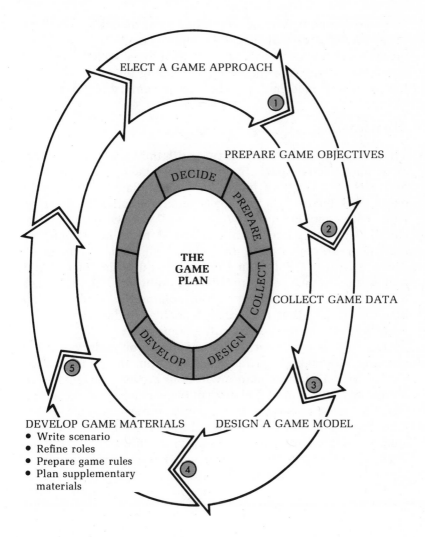

**Developing the
Game Material**

With the completion of the simulation game model, the skeleton of the final game product will have been completed. The game model must now be transferred into an interesting and playable game by creating the scenario, developing the roles, devising the rules, and incorporating the supplementary materials.

The Scenario

The scenario provides the players with the background necessary for effective participation in the game by creating a fictitious social setting in which the simulated activity will occur. A scenario has two basic characteristics: it must be sufficiently detailed to provide the players with an understanding of the game situation, and it must be sufficiently realistic and interesting to promote a high participatory level. The scenario of "Pollution Control" is quite detailed; it not only discusses the present problem of pollution, but also traces the historical development of the community. The detailed historical description of Glenbrook enables students to identify with the roles of the actors in the community.

Actors that were earlier identified can be included in the scenario although they were omitted from the game model. The inclusion of these actors will help prevent students from obtaining an oversimplified view of the way in which the actual real-life process operates. For example, the scenario for "Pollution Control" could have included the problem of the Wilson Lumber and Paper Company complying with state and federal pollution standards, but air and water pollution still being a serious problem in Glenbrook. Although not directly involved in the game activity, relevant actors, including appropriate state and federal government officials, could have been introduced.

Player Roles

In a simulation game, the students assume the roles of the actors included in the model. As discussed earlier, some actors will not be represented by players, but will be incorporated in the environmental response rules.

Actor information, obtained in the earlier stages of the design process, provides data for accurate and realistic role descriptions. Role descriptions must be accurate and realistic to insure that student behavior will correspond to the behavior of real-life actors. Each goal established in the design process should be included in the role description.

The game model will determine the types of roles. In "Pollution Control," all the actors are presented as groups and, therefore, no individual player roles are required. The single identity trait possessed by each student is his membership in a group. The game designer could have developed individual roles for the team members thus creating a more accurate representation of the real world. However, including individual roles would have raised the level of complexity unnecessarily.

Game Rules

To participate in a simulation game, all players must be familiar with basic rules. Rules are typically prepared in written form and distributed to students. Game rules are of two types: the behavioral constraint rules and the administrative rules. The behavioral constraint rules are developed in the design process and incorporated in the game model. The administrative rules prescribe the length of the play periods, the amount of time allocated to both play and administrative activity, and the mechanics of player interaction. These two types of rules are seldom presented as distinct entities in the printed game material, but are combined into a single set of game rules. The same format is followed in "Pollution Control."

Supplementary Game Material

Game scenario, role descriptions, and rules are usually printed and distributed to each student player. This material should be prepared in quantity only after the game has been pretested, since certain rules and procedures may be modified if proven unworkable in the test run. Additionally, the teacher frequently will develop his own manual containing the same information as in the player material with specific guidelines for game administration.

In certain simulation games, specific game material will be needed to make the model operable. For example, some simulation games include the element of chance, requiring a spinner or a card drawing format. Game boards may demonstrate the impact of time, space, and terrain on player moves. The requirement for specific hardware should be noted by the designer as he develops the game model. Other supplementary materials, such as name tags and signs, may lend clarity and attractiveness to the game. These, however, are not essential to the effective functioning of the simulation game. As illustrated, "Pollution Control" requires a minimum of game materials. The only materials essential to this game are copies of player rules, blackboards on which to record the outcomes of the decision stages, and identification for each player group.

The Administration of Instructional Simulations

Many teachers erroneously assume that once the simulation game is designed the difficult tasks are over, and all that remains is to relax and watch the students play. Experience indicates, however, that teachers with this attitude invariably fail to make maximum use of their simulation games. Detailed planning is needed to assure that students are properly prepared to participate, and that once in operation, the game activity progresses smoothly. The following specific areas demand teacher attention.

Time Allotments

The amount of time allotted to each play period will be determined largely by school scheduling patterns. Since many schools retain the traditional 45 or 50 minute class period, play periods generally conform to these time restraints. Schools on flexible schedules can easily provide extended periods of instruction. Under such a scheduling pattern, it may be possible for the entire simulation game to be executed during a single session. The prime advantage of continuous play is a realistic flow of events uninterrupted by artificial time segments. Some

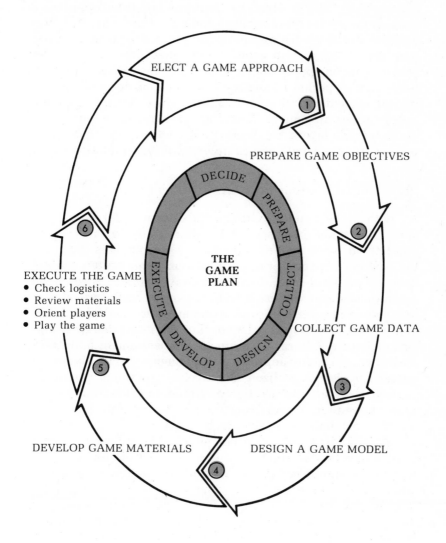

simulation games, however, are either too long or too complex to play in an uninterrupted fashion. Extended play periods can result in fatigue which invites boredom. Interrupted play enables the student to disengage and reflect upon his situation and the situations facing his fellow players. During complex and lengthy simulation games, interrupted play provides the teacher with an opportunity to analyze events with the students between play periods. Thus, the teacher's final decision regarding the breakdown of time allotments will depend upon the interrelationship among a number of factors, including the ability of the players, the degree of flexibility in the scheduling pattern, and the length and complexity of the simulation game.

Physical and Administrative Arrangements

As with all learning environments, the physical layout for simulation game play should be appropriate to the task. In addition to basic comfort factors, the teacher must consider the factor of space because simulation games often require a larger physical area than most conventional instructional techniques. Because there is frequent verbal and physical contact among players, sufficient space must be available to prevent unnecessary body contact or shouting generated by enthusiastic players. A library, learning resource room, or multi-purpose room is usually appropriate, although multiple classroom space can also be utilized effectively. If a single classroom is all that is available, an attempt should be made to find some type of temporary visual partitioning to separate teams. As a last resort, hallway space can be used.

After finding an appropriate physical location, the teacher must insure that adequate supplies are available for the duration of the simulation game. Nothing can dampen the drama and suspense generated by a simulation game more quickly than to discover that players have exhausted their supply of decision forms, and have to stop action even for a short period. If audio or video taping is to be used to record events for post-simulation game analysis, special advance arrangements are needed to secure the appropriate equipment and qualified operators.

The Selection of Administrative Assistants

The operation of a simple instructional simulation probably will not require the aid of an assistant. If the game demands extensive player activity or paperwork, however, assistance becomes mandatory. It is advisable to have too much help rather than too little until the teacher becomes more familiar with the workings of the simulation game and the types of problems that commonly occur. Preferably, the assistant should be a fellow teacher who aided in the design of the simulation game, or participated as a player during the pretest. If an inexperienced assistant must be selected, he must be briefed first in the general theory of instructional simulations, as well as in the detailed operation of the simulation game planned for use.

The assistant can be involved in a variety of ways. He can share in the necessary pre-game arrangements. During the simulation game run he can be given the responsibility for distributing and collecting player forms and insuring that they are properly executed. He can also answer procedural questions which arise during the game play, thus avoiding unnecessary delays.

The Pre-Game Briefing

Another very important step, which must be completed prior to beginning the simulation game play, is preparing the students for participation. Student attitudes toward the simulation game and the quality of the introduction they receive have been demonstrated to have a direct bearing on interest and performance levels. If the students were not involved in the design of the simulation game, or have not participated in a simulation previously, they should receive a brief introduction to the philosophy underlying the use of instructional simulations and to the basic theory behind their design and construction. Once the student understands the activity and is ready to participate, he should be given the player manual outlining the scenario, the roles, and the rules governing player activity. Some teachers prefer to distribute this information and assign roles a day or two prior to game play so the student has an opportunity to become familiar with the general structure of the simulation game, the scenario, and the roles.

Roles may be selected by the students or arbitrarily assigned by the teacher through chance drawing. Usually, self-selection is effective because a student will convincingly play a role in which he has an interest. However, if the aim of the simulation game is to increase role empathy, self-selection may not be appropriate. Some practitioners believe that if a student is required to play a role toward which he is initially hostile or indifferent, he will gain a degree of sympathy and understanding for the actor whose role he is playing. Another drawback of self-selection is that it may result in predominately strong or weak teams. Since students of like ability often associate socially, they frequently choose one another as team members. Unequal teams result in unequal competition, causing the weaker players to become demoralized. In certain cases, it is necessary for the teacher to overload some teams with capable and aggressive players. A few simulation games contain key roles that are pivotal in moving events. To insure that the game operates efficiently, these roles should be given to skilled players.

If the simulation game contains teams, the question arises as to how many players should be assigned to each team. While the answer may be partially determined by the size of the class, the teacher should realize that as the size of the team increases, the level of individual participation and interaction decreases. If the teacher finds he must assign more than five players to a team, he may be able to decrease that number by creating additional roles.

A final note of caution related to the conduct of the pre-game activity is needed. Novice leaders tend to overemphasize the importance and complexity of the simulation exercise. This may persuade students that they are about to engage in some type of mysterious experience, or one of extreme difficulty. While stressing to the students the need to follow the rules, they should not fear that a procedural error on their part will totally disrupt the simulation game. By trying to avoid mistakes, their behavior may become mechanical and unnatural. The teacher should emphasize that participation in a simulation game is an enjoyable activity, as well as a learning experience.

The Simulation Game in Operation

After all the time and effort invested in preparation, the teacher may wonder what possibly could go wrong once the game is under way. Particularly during the initial run, the teacher will probably encounter numerous problems not originally anticipated, that must be immediately resolved. Action should be taken as quickly as possible so that the flow of game activity will not be interrupted. In addition to finding immediate solutions to unexpected problems, the teacher and his assistant will be busy answering routine procedural questions. While it is impossible to adhere to precise time periods, the teacher should attempt to follow a schedule to prevent a final rush to finish each play period. The players should be told exactly how much time they will have to plan their strategies and to make their decisions.

The teacher must continuously check for intentional and unintentional rule deviations. Any major deviation by a player must be corrected if the validity of the simulation game is to be maintained. This is true also for deviations resulting from player attempts to cheat. However, frequent interruptions to correct minor unintentional errors, which probably would not affect the final outcome, would be an adverse distraction to the players and interrupt the flow of events.

Finally, the teacher must monitor the simulation game through a system of note taking for use in analyzing the completed game activity. One student may be appointed historian and given the task of keeping a running account of player interaction and decisions.

**Post-Game
Activities**

Once a simulation game has ended, two important post-game activities remain to be completed: the game discussion and the game redesign.

Post-Game Discussion

Some educators familiar with simulation games have observed that the intense involvement experienced by most students during game play precludes their reflecting objectively upon the activity. Only after the game has been completed can the teacher determine, with any degree of accuracy, what the students have learned. The accomplishment of a goal by a game player does not guarantee that he understands the logic that enabled him to attain the goal. A student can be said to have learned from the game only if he can describe the reasons for his success or failure.

During the post-game discussion, students usually are required to analyze their game strategy. If a game historian has been appointed to record the sequence of events, or if audio or video devices are used, player moves are easily recalled. From their analysis, the teacher determines how well the students have grasped the structures of the simulated process.

The post-game discussion may also include a comparison of the simulated game activity with events in real life. Such a comparison will allow students to identify the major elements of the actual process and the major defects in the game model.

Re-design of the Simulation Game

Two types of defects often become apparent during the playing of a simulation game: lack of validity and lack of playability.

There is little educational value in a simulation game which does not, at least to some degree, accurately reflect events in the real world. A simulation game based on an inaccurate model may be adversely productive since it may present a false picture of reality.

Comparison between real events and simulated events can aid in identifying invalid game rules. During the post-game discussion period, students are actually contributing to the redesign process when they find a disparity between the real and simulated activity. After a disparity has been identified, the game designer must locate the invalid assumptions which are causing players to deviate from the norm of reality, and modify it as required.

The second type of defect often found in simulation games relates to game playability. A lack of playability is often reflected in poor game play or administrative bottleneck. Players may be confused by game rules that are too complex, causing

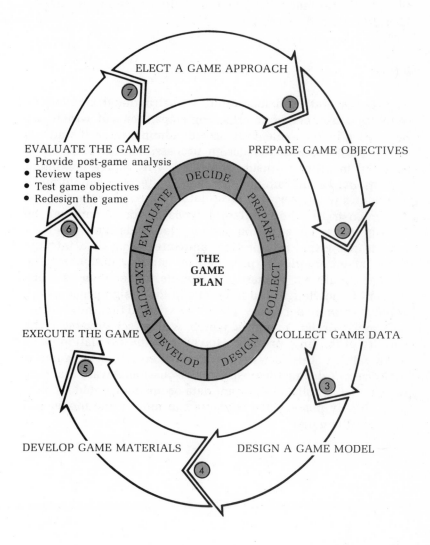

ELECT A GAME APPROACH

7

PREPARE GAME OBJECTIVES

EVALUATE THE GAME
- Provide post-game analysis
- Review tapes
- Test game objectives
- Redesign the game

6

2

DECIDE

PREPARE

EVALUATE

THE
GAME
PLAN

EXECUTE

COLLECT

DEVELOP

DESIGN

EXECUTE THE GAME

5

COLLECT GAME DATA

3

DEVELOP GAME MATERIALS

4

DESIGN A GAME MODEL

the teacher to interrupt the game play to interpret the misun-
derstood rules. Such defects are, for the most part, easily identified by the teacher and students and often corrected by merely
changing a word or phrase.

Replay

The design and implementation of instructional simulations
involves a number of interlocking steps, none of which can
be omitted by the game designer and administrator. If students
are to participate in the design process, careful planning is
essential in order to insure that they will receive maximum
educational value from the exercise. The teacher should make
available a wide variety of information sources for the purpose
of demonstrating how different types of social data can be
used in theory construction and simulation design. Wide lati-
tude in gathering, interpreting, and integrating data into the
game model should be provided for student designers. The
teacher should act primarily as a guide, rather than as a dis-
penser of knowledge, and intervene in the design process only
when absolutely necessary. It can be expected that the students
will make design mistakes which will affect adversely the
validity of the final product. However, if the simulation game
lacks validity, this fact will be discovered while the game is
in process or during the post-game discussion. Aware that they
have failed to collect important data or misinterpreted the data
they already possess, the students can modify the model and
redesign the game.

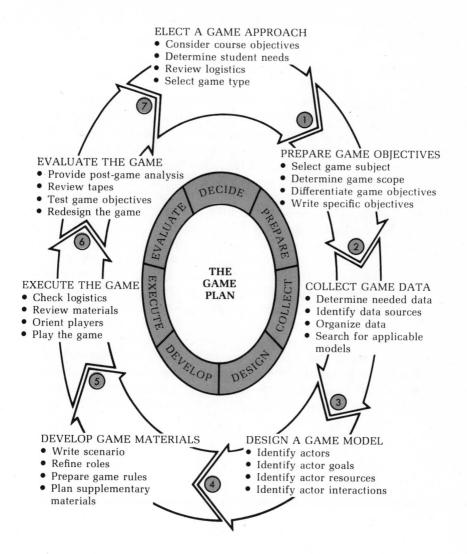

ELECT A GAME APPROACH
- Consider course objectives
- Determine student needs
- Review logistics
- Select game type

PREPARE GAME OBJECTIVES
- Select game subject
- Determine game scope
- Differentiate game objectives
- Write specific objectives

EVALUATE THE GAME
- Provide post-game analysis
- Review tapes
- Test game objectives
- Redesign the game

COLLECT GAME DATA
- Determine needed data
- Identify data sources
- Organize data
- Search for applicable models

EXECUTE THE GAME
- Check logistics
- Review materials
- Orient players
- Play the game

DECIDE
PREPARE
COLLECT
DESIGN
DEVELOP
EXECUTE
EVALUATE

THE GAME PLAN

DEVELOP GAME MATERIALS
- Write scenario
- Refine roles
- Prepare game rules
- Plan supplementary materials

DESIGN A GAME MODEL
- Identify actors
- Identify actor goals
- Identify actor resources
- Identify actor interactions

Pollution Control— A Community Political Decision-Making Simulation Game

The purpose of the simulation game "Pollution Control" is to demonstrate how political decisions are made in a typical community in the United States. The issues of "Pollution Control" are used as a vehicle for illustrating the ways in which the political decision-making process operates. The general game activity involves the Ad Hoc Committee on Air and Water Pollution Control attempting to persuade the Glenbrook City Council to enact a stringent pollution control ordinance, preferably at no cost to the general public. Opposing the Ad Hoc Committee is the Wilson Lumber and Paper Company, guilty of producing most of the air and water pollution in Glenbrook. The company will attempt to dissuade the city council from passing any type of pollution control measure, especially one that will require the company to pay for the installation and maintenance of the control system.

The Ad Hoc Committee alone does not possess sufficient influence to persuade the city council to pass the ordinance it desires, and therefore must seek support from other influential groups within the community. The Wilson Lumber and Paper Company must prevent such a coalition from forming, by persuading these influential groups that their specific goals can best be achieved by supporting its position on the pollution problem. The members of each community group will decide whether to support the Ad Hoc Committee or whether to support the Wilson Lumber and Paper Company. Their decision will be based upon the position they believe will best enable them to achieve their own social and economic goals.

The game will be played in four separate stages, with each stage corresponding to one of the four general steps in the decision-making process. These stages are:

1. *Definition of the Problem.* The problem of pollution in the community of Glenbrook is recognized and defined by the Ad Hoc Committee on Air and Water Pollution Control.

2. *Recognition of the Issue.* The problem of pollution either receives enough attention from within the community to assure some type of city council action or it does not, in which case the game ends.

3. *Formulation of Policy.* The Ad Hoc Committee on Air and Water Pollution Control and the Wilson Lumber and Paper Company submit specific policy proposals to the city council for consideration.

4. *Selection of Policy.* The city council enacts the policy proposal that elicits the most support from the community groups.

Students will be assigned to one of eight teams representing the various groups in Glenbrook who are involved in deciding the issue of pollution control. The role of each actor can be played by one or more students, although it is suggested that no more than five students be assigned to any one team, since teams that are too large decrease student interaction and participation.

The learning objectives of "Pollution Control" are:

1. An understanding of the relationship between the possession of certain types and quantities of political resources, and the ability to influence political behavior.
2. An understanding of the need to adjust political goals for the purpose of attracting political support.

3. The application of the game model in the analysis of similar political decision-making situations found in case studies.
4. The formulation of logical arguments, either for or against the enactment of pollution control legislation, in other cases dealing with the pollution problem.

Procedures
and
Rules

Stage 1
Definition of Problem Area

Action—Time Sequence

Action	*Time Allocated*
The Ad Hoc Committee on Air and Water Pollution Control and the Wilson Lumber and Paper Company formulate arguments for and against the passage of an air and water pollution control measure by the Glenbrook City Council.	Approximately 45 minutes. This stage can be completed one or two days before the game actually begins.

Narrative Description

Before a situation is recognized as a problem, it must be explicitly stated and defined by some individual or group, either within or without the community. In this game, the problem of pollution will be stated formally by the Ad Hoc Committee on Air and Water Pollution Control in the form of a written policy paper that emphasizes the deleterious impact that pollution is having upon the community of Glenbrook. At the same time, the Wilson Lumber and Paper Company, aware that the Ad Hoc Committee is planning to launch a community campaign to persuade the city council to enact a pollution control measure, will prepare its own position paper containing arguments about the adverse effect that pollution control will have upon the economic prosperity of Glenbrook. These papers will serve as a basis for negotiation during the next stage. Sufficient copies of these papers should be available to the students prior to the beginning of the next stage.

Stage 2
Recognition of the Issue

Action—Time Sequence

Action	Time Allocated
Members of the Ad Hoc Committee attempt to convince other community groups to use their resources to influence public opinion. Members of the Wilson Lumber and Paper Company contact the same groups in order to persuade them not to use their resources for the benefit of the Ad Hoc Committee.	35 minutes
Each community group decides either to use its resources to increase community interest in the pollution problem or to withhold its resources. Those groups deciding to use their resources to increase community interest will notify the Ad Hoc Committee of their decision.	10 minutes
The Ad Hoc Committee announces the total resource amount it was able to secure in its campaign to increase community interest in the pollution problem.	5 minutes

Narrative Description

Before the Glenbrook City Council will act upon the problem of pollution, it first must be convinced that a certain degree of interest in the problem exists within the community. The ability to generate community interest depends primarily upon the possession and use of two resources: reputation and ability to publicize. A resource is any tangible or intangible attribute or commodity which an actor finds useful in influencing behavior. The amount of a particular type or collection of resources an actor possesses will determine the amount of influence he is able to exert.

Below is a listing of the community groups in "Pollution Control" and a quantitative expression of their relevant resources in this stage. Their amount of resources depends upon their reputation and their ability to publicize. Their total resource points are expressed as a product of these two attributes. The figure 1 denotes low resource possession, 3 denotes medium resource possession, and 5 denotes high resource possession.

RESOURCES

Group	Reputation		Ability to Publicize	Total Resources
Wilson Lumber and Paper Company	5	×	3	15
The Ad Hoc Committee	3	×	3	9
The Paper Workers Amalgamated	3	×	1	3
The Joplin Fish Company	3	×	3	9
The First City Bank	1	×	5	5
The Chamber of Commerce	3	×	3	9
The Daily Chronicle	5	×	5	25
The Committee of Concerned Citizens for Lower Taxes	3	×	3	9

It is assumed that when a total of 30 resource points are expended by the community groups in attempting to influence public opinion, the members of the city council will realize that there exists sufficient interest in the problem of pollution to place the question on their agenda for discussion and resolution.

The general activity in this stage involves the Ad Hoc Committee attempting to convince the other community groups to use their resources to increase community interest in the problem of pollution. The Wilson Lumber and Paper Company will attempt to convince the other community groups not to use their resources for this purpose. Representatives from both the Ad Hoc Committee and the Wilson Company will personally contact the members of these groups to try to persuade them to adopt their respective courses of action. If representatives of the Ad Hoc Committee and the Wilson Company contact the same group simultaneously, the members of the contacted group will decide which representatives to see first. Representatives of the Ad Hoc Committee and representatives of the Wilson Lumber and Paper Company will distribute copies of their respective position papers to the team members of each group. After the bargaining period has ended, each community group will decide by majority vote whether or not to adopt the course of action advocated by the Ad Hoc Committee. This decision will be based on whether, in their opinion, pollution control will help them realize their social and economic goals. If the group decides to support the Ad Hoc Committee, it will present the Committee with a note containing a brief statement of its support. If the group decides not to support the Committee, it will do nothing. After the notes have been delivered to the Ad Hoc Committee, the Committee will tabulate the total amount of resources received. If the total amount is 30 or above, the Ad Hoc Committee will be assured that the issue will receive consideration by the city council and the game will progress to the next stage. If thirty resource points are not obtained for the purpose of increasing community interest, the game will terminate and the Wilson Lumber and Paper Company will be declared the winner.

Stage 3
Formulation of Policy

Action—Time Sequence

Action	*Time Allocated*
The Ad Hoc Committee on Air and Water Pollution Control and the Wilson Lumber and Paper Company each choose two policy alternatives for submission to the city council for decision.	15 minutes. This may be accomplished while other class activities are in progress.

Narrative Description

Most city councils are composed of elected lay citizens who perform their public duties on a part-time basis only. Unless a particular issue has been considered previously, it is doubtful that the individual council members will have the necessary expertise to formulate a realistic and workable pollution control policy without outside assistance. In Glenbrook, the issue of pollution is new and the only two groups that possess the resources in the form of expertise needed by the city council to formulate a pollution control policy are the Ad Hoc Committee on Air and Water Pollution Control and the Wilson Lumber and Paper Company. Thus, these two groups are the only two that are able to exert influence on the city council's decision in this stage. The Ad Hoc Committee and the Wilson Company choose two policy alternatives each from a list of thirteen for submission to the city council. It is assumed that the alternatives chosen were actually formulated by the two groups. In making their choices, the two groups must consider two things. First, they should choose alternatives that will best help them achieve their initial goals. Second, their choice must take into consideration the goals of the other community groups, since the support of these groups will be required in the next stage to help persuade the city council to enact the desired policy proposal. The alternatives from which the Ad Hoc Committee and the Wilson Company must choose and the consequences of these alternatives are listed below.

Alternative 1.　The installation of pollution control equipment that will result in a 100% reduction of air and water pollution. The cost of this equipment is $100,000 to be paid by the Wilson Lumber and Paper Company. The adoption of this policy will result in a decrease in the profits of the Wilson Company of 10% over a ten-year period and an elimination of 500 jobs. If this policy is adopted, the profits of the Joplin Fish Company will increase by $5,000 a year and Phillips Lake will be usable for recreational purposes. All foul odors will be eliminated.

Alternative 2.　The same as Alternative 1 except that the city of Glenbrook will pay for the installment of the equipment, resulting in a 5% increase in property taxes.

Alternative 3.　The installation of pollution control equipment which will result in a 50% reduction of air and water pollution. The cost of this equipment is $75,000 to be paid by the Wilson Company. The adoption of this policy will result in a decrease of 7½% in the profits of the Wilson Company over a ten-year period and an elimination of 400 jobs. If this policy is adopted, the profits of the Joplin Fish Company will increase by $5,000 a year, although Phillips Lake still will not be usable for recreational purposes. The odor emitted by the Wilson Company will be less noticeable.

Alternative 4.　The same as Alternative 3 except that the city of Glenbrook will pay for the installation of the equipment, resulting in an increase of 4% in property taxes.

Alternative 5.　The installation of pollution control equipment which will result in a 100% reduction of air pollution only. The cost of this equipment is $50,000 to be paid by the Wilson Company. The adoption of this policy will result in a decrease of 5% in the profits of the Wilson Company over a ten-year period and elimination of 250 jobs. There will be no increase in profits for the Joplin Fish Company and Phillips Lake will not be usable for recreational purposes. All odor will be eliminated.

Alternative 6.   The same as Alternative 5 except that the city of Glenbrook will pay for the installation of the equipment, resulting in an increase of 3% in property taxes.

Alternative 7.   The installation of pollution control equipment which will result in a 100% reduction of water pollution. The cost of this equipment is $50,000 to be paid by the Wilson Company. The adoption of this policy will result in a decrease of 5% in the profits of the Wilson Company over a ten-year period and an elimination of 250 jobs. The profits of the Joplin Fish Company will increase by $5,000 a year. Phillips Lake will be usable for recreational purposes. There will be no change in the level of odor emitted by the Wilson Company.

Alternative 8.   The same as Alternative 7 except that the city of Glenbrook will pay for the installation of the equipment, resulting in an increase of 3% in property taxes.

Alternative 9.   The installation of pollution control equipment which will result in a 50% reduction in air pollution. The cost of this equipment is $25,000 to be paid by the Wilson Company. The adoption of this policy will result in a 2½% decrease in the profits of the Wilson Company over a ten-year period and an elimination of 125 jobs. There will be no increase in the profits of the Joplin Fish Company and Phillips Lake will not be usable for recreational purposes. The reduction in air pollution odor will not be significant enough to be noticed by the residents of Glenbrook.

Alternative 10.   The same as Alternative 9 except that the city of Glenbrook will pay for the installation of the pollution control equipment, resulting in an increase of 2% in property taxes.

Alternative 11.   The installation of pollution control equipment which will result in a 50% reduction of water pollution. The cost of this equipment is $25,000 to be paid by the Wilson

Company. The adoption of this policy will result in a 2½% decrease in the profits of the Wilson Company over a ten-year period and an elimination of 125 jobs. There will be an increase of $5,000 yearly in the profits of the Joplin Fish Company, although Phillips Lake still will not be usable for recreational purposes. There will be no effect on the level of the odor caused by air pollution.

Alternative 12. The same as Alternative 11 except that the city of Glenbrook will pay for the installation of the pollution control equipment, resulting in an increase of 2% in property taxes.

Alternative 13. The installation of no air or water pollution control equipment. The adoption of this policy will result in no decrease in the profits of the Wilson Company and no elimination of jobs. The Joplin Fish Company will experience no increase in profits and Phillips Lake will be unusable for recreational purposes. The foul odor will remain.

Stage 4
The Selection of Policy

Action—Time Sequence

Action	*Time Allocated*
The teacher announces the policy choices selected by the Ad Hoc Committee and the Wilson Lumber and Paper Company for submission to the city council.	5 minutes
The members of the Ad Hoc Committee and the Wilson Lumber and Paper Company attempt to convince the other community groups to use their resources to influence	20 minutes

the behavior of the city council
members by persuading them to
adopt one of their respective proposals.

Each community group decides   10 minutes
which policy proposal it will support.

Each community group announces   10 minutes
the policy it will support. The policy proposal backed by the most
resources will be the one enacted
by the city council.

Narrative Description

During this last stage, the Glenbrook City Council will
enact one of the policy alternatives presented to it by the Ad
Hoc Committee or by the Wilson Company. The city council
will enact that policy that is most strongly supported by the
community groups in Glenbrook.

All the community groups are not able to exert the same
amount of influence upon the city council because they possess
different amounts of political resources. Some are politically
more powerful than others. The following is a list of the community groups and their respective resources expressed in
quantitative terms from 1, signifying very little influence, to
10, signifying a great deal of influence. Although specific types
of resources were important in stages two and three, all resources are important in stage four. For this reason, each community group is given a total number of resource points to
represent the total amount of all types of resources. The policy
proposal backed by the most resources will be the one enacted
by the city council.

Group	Total Resources
Wilson Lumber and Paper Company	10
The Ad Hoc Committee	5
The Paper Workers Amalgamated	3
The Joplin Fish Company	5

The First City Bank	8
The Chamber of Commerce	8
The Daily Chronicle	8
The Committee of Concerned Citizens for Lower Taxes	5

The general activity in this stage will be the same as that which occurred in stage two. Members of the Ad Hoc Committee and the Wilson Lumber and Paper Company will contact other community groups, and try to convince them to use their influence to help persuade the city council to enact the policy proposals they favor. The members of each group will agree among themselves to support a particular policy, and then the group will announce its choice. The policy proposal that is most strongly supported will be assumed to be the one enacted by the city council.

Game Scenario

The History of Glenbrook.   Glenbrook is a small city of 50,000 inhabitants located in the north central part of Wisconsin. It lies in a heavily forested area at the junction of Eagle River and Phillips Lake. Until about twenty years ago, this community had been relatively isolated from the outside world, connected with neighboring Smith City by a narrow two-lane highway. During heavy snows, this thirty-five mile artery is often closed for weeks at a time. Today, however, Glenbrook is connected with Smith City by a modern four-lane highway which is usable in all types of weather.

Glenbrook was founded in 1856 by Mr. Joshua Wilson, who left his native Pennsylvania to seek his fortune in the west. He had heard rumors of large sums of money being made by fur trappers operating along the rivers and lakes of Wisconsin. Upon reaching Wisconsin, Mr. Wilson happily discovered that these stories were true, and it was not long before he accumulated considerable cash reserves. Mr. Wilson, who had

been a small businessman back in Pennsylvania, put his previous experience to work. Seeking a business enterprise in
which he could profitably invest his money, he decided upon
the lumber industry. This choice was a good one, for this area
of Wisconsin abounded with some of the finest timber in the
nation. In 1856, Mr. Wilson established a small sawmill at the
mouth of the Eagle River and hired a half dozen lumberjacks
to begin cutting timber. The cut timber was floated across
Phillips Lake to the rail line which connected Smith City with
the state capital.

With the outbreak of the Civil War and the increasing
demand for timber for use in the construction of Union ships,
business boomed for the Wilson Lumber Company. War con-
tracts soon made Mr. Wilson a wealthy man, and like all good
businessmen, he eagerly reinvested his profits in the business.
As production expanded and the size of the work force increased, a small self-sustaining community grew up around
the sawmill.

With the Union victory in 1865, demand for timber began
to decline. But Mr. Wilson, ever watchful for new business
opportunities, expanded his plant and began the production
of paper. The Wilson Company became the Wilson Lumber
and Paper Company.

For the rest of the nineteenth century, the Wilson Lumber
and Paper Company and the community of Glenbrook continued to grow. The Joplin Fish Company, which found Phillips
Lake rich in fresh water fish, was the only significant new
industry to locate in Glenbrook. Because contact with the
outside world was limited, there developed within Glenbrook
a stable social structure. At the top of the social pyramid were
found the community's political, economic, and social notables.
These individuals, drawn from a dozen old established families,
had traditionally dominated the political, economic, and social
life of the community. Although community elections were
always held, there was seldom any question of who the real
political decision-makers in the community were and who
would be elected.

Under this ruling heirarchy was found a small middle class
composed almost entirely of small businessmen and shop-

keepers. A few professionals, such as physicians and attorneys, were also included. The members of this class had very little influence in the social affairs of the community and even less to say about what political decisions were made. At the bottom of the social pyramid were the blue collar workers who comprised almost 90 percent of the total population of Glenbrook. The great majority of these workers were employed by the Wilson Lumber and Paper Company, and since their personal economic security was dependent upon the good will of the company, they had no inclination to challenge the existing power structure. Most of the workers readily yielded to the political, economic, and social notables within the community.

Until the Second World War, the community changed very little. But during the war, outside forces began to impinge upon Glenbrook which were beyond the control of the ruling elite. Smith City, which was located only thirty-five miles away, had grown considerably between 1941 and 1945 and had become a major center for the production of defense related electronic equipment. The Smith City population increased from 80,000 persons in 1941 to 150,000 in 1945. As scientists poured into Smith City seeking employment, a serious housing shortage occurred. Many of these new inhabitants, unable to find homes in Smith City, settled in Glenbrook and commuted to work.

These new citizens were looked upon with a certain degree of distrust by the older residents with whom they had very little in common. The older inhabitants had an average of twelve years of schooling and an average yearly income of approximately $6,800. They were also conservative Republicans who favored the status quo, and were economically tied to the Wilson Lumber and Paper Company. In contrast, the newer residents were, for the most part, professional scientists who held at least a baccaluareate degree, had an average income of $9,500, were mostly liberal Democrats who favored progressive policies, and were economically independent of the Wilson Lumber and Paper Company.

Throughout the 1950s and 1960s Smith City continued to grow and an increasing number of its working force sought residence in Glenbrook. But despite this large influx of the new liberally oriented citizens, the traditional power structure still remains intact today and continues to closely resemble Glenbrook as it was at the turn of the century.

The Problem of Pollution in Glenbrook.   Ever since the Wilson Lumber and Paper Company began the production of paper at the close of the Civil War, chemicals that were used in the manufacturing process were eliminated by dumping them into Eagle River and Phillips Lake. Until recently, this was the cause of little concern because of the level of pollution was not great enough to affect the quality or quantity of the fish caught in the lake, and thus did not adversely affect the prosperity of the Joplin Fish Company. It had always been assumed that there existed no solution to the pollution problem, since residual chemical materials were inevitable and the only place to dispose of them was into the water. However, as the population of Glenbrook grew during the 1950s and 1960s, homes began to spring up along the banks of the river and the lake. Most of these new homes belonged to the scientists who worked in Smith City. They became worried when they found that prolonged exposure to this water caused severe and painful skin irritation. However, water pollution was not the only concern of these citizens. Many of the new homes were located downwind from the Company and were regularly exposed to the rotten egg odor which was emitted from its smokestacks. Because the level of pollution had increased during recent years, the Joplin Fish Company discovered that fish were dying off which was resulting in a decline in profits.

A new group, composed primarily of these new home owners, was recently organized for the purpose of forcing the Glenbrook City Council to enact some type of pollution control ordinance. As this newly formed Ad Hoc Committee on Air and Water Pollution Control was organizing and planning its strategy, the Wilson Lumber and Paper Company got word of what was happening and began to devise a counter strategy. Both groups realize that they will have to go out and actively seek support from other influential individuals and groups within the community. They must be persuaded to use their influence to either help or hinder the passage of a pollution control ordinance by the City Council.

Role Descriptions

Board of Directors, Wilson Lumber and Paper Company

You are a member of the Board of Directors of the Wilson Lumber and Paper Company and, as such, one of the most respected and powerful individuals in the community of Glenbrook. Your company employs well over half of the working force of the city and is the principal economic institution in the community. You realize that your company has been polluting the air and water, but until recently you thought very little about it because the problem was of little concern to the general public. Now some opinions are changing, and for the first time in the history of Glenbrook, your company is being attacked by residents of the community. You oppose the installation of pollution control devices for economic reasons. During the past few years profits have gradually declined, and the installation and operation of a costly pollution control system could further depress the company's earnings. A reduction in profits might possibly result in having to lay off some of the company's employees. You firmly believe that the economic health of the community is dependent upon the operation of your company as it has in the past. Your goal is to prevent the enactment of any type of pollution control measure for which you will have to pay.

Officers of the Ad Hoc Committee on Air and Water Pollution Control

You are one of the officers of the Ad Hoc Committee on Air and Water Pollution Control. Your committee was just recently organized for the purpose of forcing the enactment of a regulation by the Glenbrook City Council, to stop the Wilson Lumber and Paper Company from polluting the air and water with its waste materials. Your organization is composed primarily of young professional scientists who live in

Glenbrook but who work in Smith City. You realize that your
opponent is indeed formidable, and that your fight will be
uphill all the way. But you are dedicated to your task, and
will pursue it until the goal is accomplished or until all alternative options have been explored and rejected. Your goal is
to persuade the Glenbrook City Council to enact a very
stringent pollution control ordinance at minimal cost to the
public.

Board of Directors, The
First City Bank

You are a member of the Board of Directors of the First
City Bank, the only bank in Glenbrook. Your bank is involved
in most all of the financial activity in the community, and
holds a monopoly on money transactions and credit grants.
You are highly respected within the community and have many
friends among the political, economic, and social elite. Your
contacts with the Wilson Lumber and Paper Company are
particularly close. The First City Bank was organized just five
years after Mr. Wilson established his first sawmill, and since
that time the two institutions have cooperated very closely
in planning and directing the economic and financial life of
the community. Your goal is to insure the continued economic
prosperity of Glenbrook.

Board of Directors, Chamber
of Commerce

You are a member of the Board of Directors of the Glenbrook Chamber of Commerce. Since its founding in 1901, your
organization has been very active in community affairs, particularly in recruiting small businessmen to Glenbrook. Your
advertising campaign in the state has attempted to show Glenbrook as an economically strong community full of promise
for future development. The Chamber has been traditionally
conservative, but has not hesitated in recommending bold
action when it was thought that such action was in the community's best interest. Your organization is composed of a cross-

section of the Glenbrook business community; from the small corner grocer to the members of the Board of Directors of the Wilson Lumber and Paper Company. Your goal is to insure the continued economic prosperity of Glenbrook, but at the same time make it a satisfying community in which to live.

The Board of Editors, The Daily Chronicle

You are a member of the Board of Editors of the Daily Chronicle, the only local mass circulation newspaper within the community. Because of the monopoly the Daily Chronicle holds over the distribution and interpretation of the news, you are one of the principal opinion-makers within Glenbrook, and have very close personal contact with the other political, economic, and social notables in the community. Your goal is to insure the continued prosperity of the economy of Glenbrook, but at the same time make it a satisfying community in which to live.

Officers, The Joplin Fish Company

For over a hundred years Phillips Lake has provided your company with a large yearly catch of fish. Although the lake has always been used as a dumping ground for the Wilson Lumber and Paper Company's pollution, until recently the level has not been high enough to adversely affect the size of the yield. During recent years as the level of pollution has risen, your profits have correspondingly declined. Your goal is to convince the City Council to reduce the level of water pollution in Phillips Lake to a point where it will no longer have an adverse effect on your fish production.

Officers, The Paper Workers, Amalgamated

Your organization represents the interest of the workers who are employed by the Wilson Lumber and Paper Company.

Since the establishment of your union in 1952, there have been very few major conflicts with the management of the Wilson Company, and those conflicts that did arise were resolved without resorting to strike action. The economic security of your membership is closely linked with the continued prosperity of the Wilson Company. Your goal is to work for the continued material well-being of the Wilson Lumber and Paper Company workers.

Officers, The Committee of Concerned Citizens for Lower Taxes

The main objective of your organization is to reduce all nonessential government spending in Glenbrook. You consider your committee to be the only effective watchdog over government spending. Your goal is to oppose an increase in spending that you feel is not essential for the well-being of the community of Glenbrook.

A Simulation Game Response Sheet

The text has emphasized simulation game design and execution skills. An open-ended response sheet and checklist is provided as (1) a review of the major tasks in game construction, or (2) a set of key questions for teachers electing to prepare a classroom simulation. Although appropriate responses to these key items will not guarantee game success, the avoidance of some pitfalls is probable and a systematic approach is assured.

(1) *What Specific Learning Objectives Will Be Realized Thru the Simulation?*

    (1.1)

    (1.2)

    (1.3)

    (1.4)

    (1.5)

(2) What Specific Logistical Concerns Must Be Resolved Prior
to the Simulation?

Time Concerns

(2.1)

(2.2)

(2.3)

Space Concerns

(2.4)

(2.5)

(2.6)

Talent Concerns

(2.7)

(2.8)

(2.9)

(3) *Have the Following Specific Tasks Been Performed?*

(3.1) ____Prepare specific objectives for the game

(3.2) ____Determine the scope of the game

(3.3) ____Identify data sources

(3.4) ____Collect and organize data

(3.5) ____Design a game model

(3.6) ____Identify actors, resources, and interactions

(3.7) ____Write a scenario

(3.8) ____Develop game rules

(3.9) ____Prepare supplementary materials

(3.10) ____Assign roles

(4) *Has Adequate Preparation Been Made for Playing the Game?*

    (4.1) ____Re-check time and space factors

    (4.2) ____Select assistants, game historian

    (4.3) ____Check supply of materials and forms

    (4.4) ____Orient players to roles and scenario

    (4.5) ____Provide for audio and/or visual recording of game-in-progress

(5) *Have Certain Actions Been Anticipated Should Events Not Flow Appropriately During the Game Play?*

Playing Schedule Interruptions

(5.1)

Rule Deviations

(5.2)

Monitoring Problems

(5.3)

Other Contingency Plans

(5.4)

(6) *Has an Appropriate Post-Game Analysis Been Planned?*

 (6.1) ____Vocal critique

 (6.2) ____Written critique

 (6.3) ____Content level analysis

 (6.4) ____Feeling level analysis

 (6.5) ____Task level analysis

 (6.6) ____Surface agenda items

 (6.7) ____Hidden agenda items

 (6.8) ____Audio and/or visual replay

 (6.9) ____Game historian report

 (6.10) ____Teacher observations

(7) *What Were the Outcomes of the Simulation Game?*

Stated Outcomes

 (7.1)

 (7.2)

 (7.3)

Implied Outcomes

 (7.4)

 (7.5)

 (7.6)

(8) *How Can the Game Be Improved?*

Scenario Changes

 (8.1)

 (8.2)

 (8.3)

Role Modifications

 (8.4)

(8.5)

(8.6)

Material Improvements

(8.7)

(8.8)

(8.9)

Rule Changes

(8.10)

(8.11)

(8.12)

Logistical Recommendations

(8.13)

(8.14)

(8.15)

Other Needed Changes

(8.16)

(8.17)

(8.18)

(9) Did the Game Experience Produce the Pre-Game Learning Objectives?

Evidences of Satisfying Objectives

(9.1)

(9.2)

(9.3)

(9.4)

Evidences of Not Satisfying Objectives

(9.5)

(9.6)

(9.7)

Possible Explanations for Objectives Not Met

(9.8)

(9.9)

appendix c

Bibliography

Books

Abt, Clark C. *Serious Games*. New York: The Viking Press, 1970.

Boocock, Sarane S. and E. O. Schild (eds.). *Simulation Games in Learning*. Beverly Hills, California: Sage Publications, Inc., 1968.

Carlson, Elliot. *Learning Through Games*. Washington, D. C.: Public Affairs Press, 1969.

Giffin, Sidney F. *The Crises Game: Simulating International Conflict*. Garden City, New York: Doubleday and Company, 1965.

Gordon, Alice Kaplan. *Games for Growth: Educational Games in the Classroom*. Palo Alto, California: Science Research Associates, Inc., 1970.

Guetzkow, Harold et al. *Simulation in International Relations: Developments for Research and Teaching*. Englewood Cliffs, New Jersey: Prentice-Hall, Inc., 1963.

_____. et al. *Simulation in Social and Administrative Science: Overviews and Case Examples*. Englewood Cliffs, New Jersey: Prentice-Hall, Inc., 1972.

Inbar, Michael and Clarice S. Stoll (eds.). *Simulation and Gaming in Social Science*. New York: The Free Press, 1972.

85

Nesbitt, William A. *Simulation Games for the Social Studies Classroom (2nd Edition)*. New York: Foreign Policy Association, 1971.

Raser, John R. *Simulation and Society*. Boston, Massachusetts: Allyn and Bacon, 1969.

Zukerman, David and Robert Horn. *The Guide to Simulation Games for Education and Training*. Cambridge, Massachusetts: Information Resources, Inc., 1970.

ARTICLES

Anderson, C. Raymond. "An Experiment in Behavioral Learning in a Consumer Credit Game," *Simulation and Games* 1 no. 1 (March 1970), 43-54.

Boocock, Sarane S. "An Experimental Study of the Learning Effects of Two Games with Simulated Environments," *American Behavioral Scientist* 10, no. 2 (October 1966), 8-17.

_____. "The Life Career Game," *The Personnel and Guidance Journal* 46, no. 4 (December 1967), 328-334.

_____. "Using Simulation Games in College Courses," *Simulation and Games* 1, no. 1 (March 1970), 67-79.

_____ and James S. Coleman. "Games with Simulated Environments in Learning," *Sociology of Education* 39, no. 3 (Summer 1966), 215-236.

Bloomfield, Lincoln P. "Political Gaming," *United States Naval Institute Proceedings* 86 (September 1960), 57-64.

_____ and Norman J. Padelford. "Three Experiments in Political Gaming," *American Political Science Review* 53, no. 4 (December 1959), 1105-1115.

Braskamp, Larry A. and Richard M. Hodgetts. "The Role of an Objective Evaluation Model in Simulation Gaming," *Simulation and Games* 2, no. 2 (June 1971), 197-212.

Burgess, Phillip M. et al. "Organizing Simulated Environments," *Social Education* 33, no. 2 (February 1969), 185-192.

Chartier, Myron R. "Learning Effect: An Experimental Study of a Simulation Game and Instrumented Discussion," *Simulation and Games* 3, no. 2 (June 1972), 203-218.

Cherryholmes, Cleo H. "Some Current Research on Effectiveness of Educational Simulations: Implications for Alternative Strategies," *American Behavioral Scientist* 10, no. 2 (October 1966), 4-7.

Clarke, Wentworth. "A Research Note on Simulation in the Social Studies," *Simulation and Games* 1, no. 2 (June 1970), 203-210.

Cohen, Bernard C. "Political Gaming in the Classroom," *The Journal of Politics* 24, no. 2 (May 1962), 367-381.

DeKock, Paul. "Simulations and Changes in Racial Attitudes," *Social Education* 33, no. 2 (February 1969), 181-183.

Druckman, Daniel. "Understanding the Operation of Complex Social Systems: Some Uses of Simulation Design," *Simulation and Games* 2, no. 2 (June 1971), 173-195.

Fletcher, Jerry L. "The Effectiveness of Simulation Games as Learning Environments," *Simulation and Games* 2, no. 4 (December 1971), 425-454.

Gillespie, Judith A. "Analyzing and Evaluating Classroom Games," *Social Education* 36, no. 1 (January 1972), 33-42.

Goldhammer, Herbert, and Hans Speier. "Some Observations on Political Gaming," *World Politics* 12, no. 1 (October 1959), 71-83.

Heap, James L. "The Student as Resource: Uses of the Minimum-Structure Simulation Game in Teaching," *Simulation and Games* 2, no. 4 (December 1971), 473-487.

Inbar, Michael. "The Differential Impact of a Game Simulating a Community Disaster," *American Behavioral Scientist* 10, no. 2 (October 1966), 18-27.

Kardatzke, Howard. "Simulation Games in the Social Studies: The 'Reality' Issue," *Social Education* 33, no. 2 (February 1969), 179-180.

Kraft, Ivor. "Pedagogical Futility in Fun and Games?" *The Journal of the National Education Association* 56, no. 1 (January 1967), 71-72.

Lee, Robert S., and Arlene O'Leary. "Attitudes and Personality Effects of a Three-day Simulation," *Simulation and Games* 2, no. 3 (September 1971), 309-347.

Livingston, Samuel A. "Effects of a Legislative Simulation Game on the Political Attitudes of Junior High School Students," *Simulation and Games* 3, no. 1 (March 1972), 41-51.

Robinson, James A., et al. "Teaching with Inter-Nation Simulation and Case Studies," *American Political Science Review* 60, no. 1 (March 1966), 53-65.

Sachs, Stephen M. "The Uses and Limits of Simulation Models in Teaching Social Science and History," *The Social Studies,* 61, no. 4 (April 1970), 163-167.

Scanlan, Eugene. "Morningside University: An Environmentally Structured Simulation," *Simulation and Games* 1, no. 4 (December 1970), 429-433.

Shubick, Martin et al. "An Artificial Player for a Business Market Game," *Simulation and Games* 2, no. 1 (March 1971), 27-43.

Stoll, Clarice S., and Michael Inbar. "Games and Socialization: An Exploratory Study of Race Differences," *The Sociological Quarterly* 11, no. 3 (Summer 1970), 374-381.

Tansey, P. J. "Simulation Techniques in the Training of Teachers,"
    Simulation and Games 1, no. 3 (September 1970), 281-303.
Twelker, Paul A. "Some Reflections on Instructional Simulations and
    Gaming," Simulation and Games 3, no. 2 (June 1972), 145-153.
Umpleby, Stuart. "The Teaching Computer as a Gaming Laboratory,"
    Simulation and Games 2, no. 1 (March 1971), 5-25.

A Select List of Commercial Simulation Games

The following are representative samples of man simulation games now available on the educational market.

International Relations

CRISIS

Description: A simulation game dealing with a fictional world crisis. Students are assigned to teams representing nations who are competing for the possession of a precious metal.

Level: Elementary school, junior high school, senior high school, and college.

Availability: Simile II, 1150 Silverado, La Jolla, California 92037.

DANGEROUS PARALLEL

Description: A game modeled on the events leading up to the outbreak of the Korean War. Students assume the roles of leaders of several fictional nations.

Level: Senior high school and college.

Availability: Scott, Foresman and Company, 1900 E. Lake Avenue, Glenview, Illinois 60025.

FOREIGN POLICY DECISION-MAKING

Description: A simulation game dealing with the complexities of the foreign policy decision-making process. Students assume roles of groups normally involved in the formulation of foreign policy.

Level: Senior high school and college.

Availability: Markham Publishing Company, 3322 West Peterson Avenue, Chicago, Illinois 60659.

GRAND STRATEGY

Description: An international relations simulation game based upon events in Europe during the period of the First World War. Students assume the roles of leaders of European nations.

Level: Senior high school and college.

Availability: Games Central, Abt Associates, Inc., 55 Wheeler Street, Cambridge, Massachusetts 02138.

INTER-NATION SIMULATION

Description: A game in which students interact as leaders of several fictional nations. Players must contend with internal and external factors in making decisions. Available in two levels of complexity for high school and college students.

Level: Senior high school and college (separate games).

Availability: Science Research Associates, Inc., 259 East Erie Street, Chicago, Illinois 60611.

THE STATE SYSTEM EXERCISE

Description: A simulation game designed to trace the evolution of the nation-state and international relations. Deals with the 18th century balance of power system, the "transitional" system of the late 19th and early 20th centuries, and the present bi-polar system.

Level: Senior high school and college.

Availability: Markham Publishing Company, 3322 West Peterson Avenue, Chicago, Illinois 60659.

Government and Politics

AMERICAN GOVERNMENT SIMULATION SERIES

Description: A group of simulation games dealing with the American Constitutional Convention, the budgetary process, presidential election campaigns, and the various aspects of the legislative process.

Level: Senior high school and college.

Availability: Science Research Associates, Inc., 259 East Erie Street, Chicago, Illinois 60611.

CAMPAIGN

Description: A political simulation that treats a number of topics relating to the election of a state legislature including political party organization, the nominating process, election tactics, and election news coverage.

Level: Junior high school, senior high school, and college.

Availability: Instructional Simulations, Inc., 2147 University Avenue, St. Paul, Minnesota 55114.

DEMOCRACY

Description: A game that simulates the operation of a legislature and the variables that affect legislator behavior. This game can be played at eight different levels of complexity.

Level: Junior high school, senior high school, and college.

Availability: Western Publishing Company, Inc., School and Library Department, 150 Parish Drive, Wayne, New Jersey 07470.

SITTE

Description: A community political decision-making simulation game. Students assume the roles of members of five interest groups attempting to influence the outcome of community decisions.

Level: Junior high school, senior high school, and college.

Availability: Simile II, 1150 Silverado, La Jolla, California 92037.

Social Processes

COMMUNITY DISASTER

Description: A simulation game in which the participants become involved in a hypothetical community disaster. The players are confronted with the conflict between insuring the safety of their families and helping the community solve its emergency problems.

Level: Senior high school and adult.

Availability: Western Publishing Company, School and Library Department, 150 Parish Drive, Wayne, New Jersey 07470.

GENERATION GAP

Description: A simulation game dealing with the relationship between parent and child. The game activity involves the solution of five issues toward which parents and children have opposing attitudes.

Level: Junior high school and senior high school.

Availability: Western Publishing Company, School and Library Department, 150 Parish Drive, Wayne, New Jersey 07470.

LIFE CAREER

Description: The players in this simulation game must make educational and employment decisions relating to the roles of the individuals they are playing.

Level: Junior high school and senior high school.

Availability: Western Publishing Company, School and Library Department, 150 Parish Drive, Wayne, New Jersey 07470.

EDGE CITY COLLEGE

Description: A simulation game that presents various issues relating to higher education. Students assume roles of various actors found in the university community.

Level: Senior high school and college.

Availability: URBANDYNE, 5659 South Woodlawn Avenue, Chicago, Illinois 60637.

SUNSHINE

Description: Students assume various racial identities in a simulation game dealing with urban racial problems.

Level: Elementary school, junior high school, and senior high school.

Availability: Interact, P.O. Box 262, Lakeside, California 92040.

Economics

CONSUMER

Description: A simulation game dealing with credit borrowing. Students assume roles of credit consumers and credit and loan managers.

Level: Junior high school, senior high school, and adults.

Availability: Western Publishing Company, School and Library Department, 150 Parish Drive, Wayne, New Jersey 07470.

ECONOMIC DECISION GAME

Description: A series of eight games dealing with the collective bargaining, the firm, the market, the community, the scarcity and allocation, the banking, the national economy, and international trade.

Level: Twelfth grade and first year college.

Availability: Science Research Associates, Inc., 259 East Erie Street, Chicago, Illinois 60611.

ECONOMIC SYSTEM

Description: A simulation in which players assume the roles of workers, farmers, and manufacturers. Player activity involves the production, marketing, and consumption of food and manufactured goods.

Level: Junior high school, senior high school, and college.

Availability: Western Publishing Company, School and Library Department, 150 Parish Drive, Wayne, New Jersey 07470.

SETTLE OR STRIKE

Description: A simulation game dealing with the problems associated with collective bargaining. Students assume roles of union and management negotiators working with such issues as wages and contract duration.

Level: Senior high school.

Availability: Games Central, Abt Associates, Inc., 55 Wheeler Street, Cambridge, Massachusetts 02138.

SMOG

Description: An atmospheric pollution game dealing with the problem of maintaining a balance between industrial pollution and clean air.

Level: Senior high school and college.

Availability: Urban Systems, Inc., 1033 Massachusetts Avenue, Cambridge, Massachusetts 02138.

History

AMERICAN HISTORY GAMES

Description: A series of six games dealing with the economics of the Colonial period, the economic and political development of the early West, Reconstruction, industrialization and urbanization during the late 19th century, American expansionism in the late 19th and early 20th century, and contemporary international relations.

Level: Junior high school, senior high school, and first two years of college.

Availability: Science Research Associates, Inc., 259 East Erie Street, Chicago, Illinois 60611.

DESTINY

Description: In this game students assume roles of six actors who influence the course of events during the outbreak of the Spanish-American War. The actors include the Spanish diplomats, the Cuban junta, the American press, businessmen, imperialists, and anti-imperialists.

Level: Junior high school and senior high school.

Availability: Interact, P.O. Box 262, Lakeside, California 92040.

DISCOVERY

Description: A simulation game in which students play the roles of American colonists during the 17th century. The problems faced by the players include planning for colonization, selection of sites to establish colonies, decisions relating to daily survival.

Level: Fourth, fifth, and sixth grade.

Availability: Interact, P.O. Box 262, Lakeside, California 92040.

DIVISION

Description: A game that deals with the political turmoil in the United States in the decade preceding the outbreak of the Civil War. The groups represented by players are Western Republicans, Eastern Republicans, Abolitionists, Southern Democrats, Northern Democrats, and Constitutional Unionists.

Level: Junior high school and senior high school.

Availability: Interact, P.O. Box 262, Lakeside, California 92040.

NUREMBERG

Description: A simulation that recreates the International Military Tribunal at Nuremberg at the close of the Second World War. This game involves the controversial questions relating to war crimes. Students play the roles of judges, prosecuting attorneys, defense attorneys, prosecution witnesses, defense witnesses, and defendants.

Level: Junior high school and senior high school:

Availability: Interact, P.O. Box 262, Lakeside, California 92040.

Miscellaneous

KRIEGSPIEL

Description: A war game based upon skill. Players assume the roles of opposing commanders.

Level: Senior high school and adult.

Availability: The Avalon Hill Company, 4517 Harford Road, Baltimore, Maryland 21214.

MOOT

Description: A game that deals with the problems of justice. The game activity involves both civil and criminal law.

Level: Junior high school, senior high school, and college.

Availability: Interact, P.O. Box 262, Lakeside, California 92040.

SEARCH

Description: A simulation game designed to familiarize students with library resources. The game activity involves the search for information and the solving of problems requiring an understanding of the use of library resources.

Level: Junior high school and senior high school.

Availability: Interact, P.O. Box 262, Lakeside, California 92040.

Index

Values clarification thru role playing
  Boggle
  Clue
cards
convect for
hayman
risk
  panel discussion

LB1029.S53   M34   010101 000
Maidment, Robert.
Simulation games; design and i

0 2002 0096473 8
YORK COLLEGE OF PENNSYLVANIA 17403

83311

LB
1029
.S53
M34

MAIDMENT
    SIMULATION GAMES

DISCARDED

LIBRARY

18